I had the privilege of having Jeff Harshbarger as a Bible college student shortly after his deliverance from the occult. It was a thrill to watch him mature in his Christian life and then grow to the point of being able to minister to others caught in the grips of the occult. In *Dancing With the Devil*, Jeff joins with several other former occultists to bring us their spellbinding stories of their deliverance from being spellbound. This volume is far more than just intriguing true-life stories; it is a manual on how to break free from demonic chains and how to help others find true freedom through Christ. *Dancing With the Devil* is a must-read for anyone trapped on the dark side and for everyone desiring to rescue others from the shadows.

—Delron Shirley
Former Dean, Indiana Christian University
Noblesville, IN

Powerful and eye opening to the kingdom of darkness. Every Christian should read this book. We are in a real warfare, and over half of God's army is asleep.

—Cody Gunderson
Senior Pastor, Yosemite Lakes Community Church
Coarsegold, CA

The occult in all its various disguises is causing havoc around the world. Good, clear information both to explain to those caught up what is going on and to help them overcome the various issues in their life has never been more needed than it is today. It is so easy to give advice to those needing help without really understanding what they are going through. Enter Jeff Harshbarger. He is not just a talker; he has been there and knows what others are going through. This book should be a message of hope to the thousands who are looking for a way out, because it will show them they are not alone. There are compassionate people waiting to listen to their story and give practical help.

One of the most difficult aspects of being a missionary to cults and false religious movements is the resentment they have for Christians who communicate false information about their beliefs. This is most true in the area of Satanism and the occult. I have appreciated Jeff's ministry, and *Dancing With the Devil* is a helpful tool in educating Christians about the beliefs of those with these worldviews.

—LL (Don) Veinot Jr.
President, Midwest Christian Outreach, Inc.
Wonder Lake, IL

Jeff Harshbarger's *Dancing With the Devil* is a helpful and needful book because it is a unique approach to understanding occultism from a Christian point of view. Most evangelicals think of "the occult" as a vaguely defined but threatening realm of spiritual darkness and danger. Harshbarger has collected personal tales of occult involvement that bring clarity and detail to that murky image and refine our abstract impressions of "occultism" into concrete discernments of its real dangers and the real means of escaping from them. If you are dealing with occult-related issues—either in your own life or the lives of others—this book needs to be in your library.

—Brooks Alexander
Author of *Witchcraft Goes Mainstream*
and Founder of Spiritual Counterfeits Project
Berkeley, CA

Dancing With the Devil will touch your heart with compassion for those caught in the world of the occult and enrich your mind with the knowledge to help them. Jeff Harshbarger provides a fast-paced and fascinating look into the realm of the prince of darkness.

—Jill Martin Rische
Author of *The Kingdom of the Occult*

DANCING
with the DEVIL

An honest look into the occult
from former followers

COMPILED BY

Jeff Harshbarger

CHARISMA
HOUSE

Most CHARISMA HOUSE BOOK GROUP products are available at special quantity discounts for bulk purchase for sales promotions, premiums, fund-raising, and educational needs. For details, write Charisma House Book Group, 600 Rinehart Road, Lake Mary, Florida 32746, or telephone (407) 333-0600.

DANCING WITH THE DEVIL compiled by Jeff Harshbarger
Published by Charisma House
Charisma Media/Charisma House Book Group
600 Rinehart Road
Lake Mary, Florida 32746
www.charismahouse.com

Unless otherwise noted, all Scripture quotations are from the New International Version. Copyright © 1973, 1978, 1984, International Bible Society. Used by permission.

Scripture quotations marked CEV are from the Contemporary English Version, copyright © 1995 by the American Bible Society. Used by permission.

Scripture quotations marked ESV are from the Holy Bible, English Standard Version. Copyright © 2001 by Crossway Bibles, a division of Good News Publishers. Used by permission.

Scripture quotations marked KJV are from the King James Version of the Bible.

Scripture quotations marked NAS are from the New American Standard Bible, copyright © 1960, 1962, 1963, 1968, 1971, 1972, 1973, 1975, 1977, 1995 by The Lockman Foundation. Used by permission. (www.Lockman .org)

Visit the author's website at www.refugeministries.cc.

Some names, places, and identifying details with regard to stories in this book have been changed to help protect the privacy of individuals who may have been involved or had similar experiences.

Library of Congress Cataloging-in-Publication Data:

Dancing with the Devil / [edited by] Jeff Harshbarger.
    p. cm.
  Includes bibliographical references (p.   ).
  ISBN 978-1-61638-695-5 (trade paper) -- ISBN 978-1-62136-042-1 (e-book)
  1. Occultism--Religious aspects--Christianity. 2. Christian converts--Biography. I. Harshbarger, Jeff.
  BR115.O3D36 2012
  261.5'13--dc23

                  2012020523

12 13 14 15 16 — 9 8 7 6 5 4 3 2 1
Printed in the United States of America

To Harry and Jo Richardson

CONTENTS

ACKNOWLEDGMENTS

THIS BOOK COULD not have been written without the tireless efforts of my wonderful wife, Liz.

Thanks to Max the dog for teaching me true friendship.

Special thanks to Rebeca Seitz and Jessica Dotta at Reclaim Management for making this book, which I've wanted to write since 2007, a reality.

Thank you to all the contributing authors for sharing from your heart.

Thanks to all the folks at Charisma House for believing in this project.

And as always, thanks to the Lord Jesus Christ for being faithful.

PREFACE

THE OCCULT HAS permeated society throughout the world. Some of the most popular movies, television shows, and books today portray the occult in a very alluring manner. Practices such as meditation and reiki relaxation therapy, which were once considered "flaky" and countercultural, are now widely accepted. I've even known churchgoers who readily admitted to reading their horoscopes each day.

Despite the pervasive influence of the occult, many Christians are still not fully aware of what it is, how it operates, and why so many people are lured into its trap. Much false information about the occult has been circulated among Christians in recent decades. This misinformation has prevented many well-meaning Christians from relating to occultists in a loving manner and, as a result, from sharing the love of God with them.

You may think occultists live on the margins of society, but you likely know someone who is dabbling in spiritualism, the New Age, or Eastern mysticism. Chances are you've rubbed shoulders with someone who turns to psychic mediums or astrologers for insight into their future. Most occult followers are decent, law-abiding citizens who carpool their kids to school and pay their taxes on time. They don't dress weird, they make good friends, and many don't share what they practice or believe.

In 2005 I wrote a book titled *From Darkness to Light: How to Rescue Someone You Love From the Occult*. It included my testimony of how Jesus Christ delivered me from Satanism, an elementary primer on the occult, and a few testimonies from occultists who came to Christ. But it was not enough. The need for more good information was obvious.

So several friends from various occult backgrounds graciously agreed to help me write a book on the topic. They all were once ensconced in the demonic realm and have experienced the saving grace of Jesus Christ. Today they are firmly established in their faith and through their contributions to this book are offering insight into who occultists are, what they believe, and how to effectively minister to them.

Until the modern-day church recognizes the real face of an occult follower, it cannot serve as a source of hope and love. It cannot introduce the intimacy of redemption to someone it does not know. Allow this book to arm you for the battle that is raging all around us. My prayer is that after reading these testimonies, you will be prepared to move forward in wisdom and love to help those caught in the crosshairs of the occult find true freedom in Christ.

Introduction

WHAT IS THE OCCULT?

THE WORD OCCULT is derived from the Latin word *occultus*, which means "hidden or secret things." Many people who entered the world of the occult were on a journey to enlightenment. They were seeking hidden knowledge that they thought would improve their lives, but somewhere along the path to wisdom they detoured and ended up enslaved to their own desires and to Satan.

According to the wisdom of popular culture, there is nothing wrong with consulting psychics or the stars, or practicing witchcraft, Wicca, transcendental meditation, psychic healing, necromancy (speaking to the dead), and the like. Hollywood would have you think these practices are not only acceptable but also good! Yet the Bible is clear about the occult. All forms of occultism are detestable to God.

> When you enter the land the Lord your God is giving you, be very careful not to imitate the detestable customs of the nations living there. For example, never sacrifice your son or daughter as a burnt offering. And do not let your people practice fortune-telling, or use sorcery, or interpret omens, or engage in witchcraft, or cast spells, or function as mediums or psychics, or call forth the spirits of the dead. Anyone who does these things is detestable to the Lord. It is because the other nations have done these detestable things that the Lord your God will drive them out ahead of you. But you must be blameless before the Lord your God. The nations you are

about to displace consult sorcerers and fortune-tellers, but the Lord your God forbids you to do such things.

—Deuteronomy 18:9–14, nlt

This is not the only warning against the occult in Scripture. For instance, in Isaiah 47:12–15 and throughout the Book of Daniel astrologers are shown to be powerless deceivers. Acts 16 shows that a demon was really behind a woman's psychic ability. And various forms of sorcery and divination are clearly condemned in Hosea 4:12, Exodus 22:18, and Isaiah 44:25. God is not fooling around when it comes to the world of the occult. He abhors such practices. Even someone who reads their horoscope in the daily newspaper is considered a practicing occultist, because he is looking to astrology for answers and direction instead of to God.

God has revealed Himself through His Son, Jesus Christ, and His Word, the Bible. There is nothing "hidden or secret" about knowing God. He has not withheld anything good from us. The lie that God is keeping something from us that would make us wiser or more powerful was formulated by Satan in the Garden of Eden.

The serpent was the shrewdest of all the wild animals the Lord God had made. One day he asked the woman, "Did God really say you must not eat the fruit from any of the trees in the garden?"

"Of course we may eat fruit from the trees in the garden," the woman replied. "It's only the fruit from the tree in the middle of the garden that we are not allowed to eat. God said, 'You must not eat it or even touch it; if you do, you will die.'"

"You won't die!" the serpent replied to the woman. "God knows that your eyes will be opened as soon as you eat it, and you will be like God, knowing both good and evil."

The woman was convinced. She saw that the tree was beautiful and its fruit looked delicious, and she wanted the wisdom it would give her. So she took some of the fruit and

ate it. Then she gave some to her husband, who was with her,
and he ate it, too.

—GENESIS 3:1–6, NLT

From this passage we see that God allowed Satan, in the guise of
the serpent, to test Adam and Eve. The serpent approached them
and challenged their knowledge and understanding of what God
had said. God laid out the ground rules in Genesis 2:16–17. He
warned Adam: "You may freely eat the fruit of every tree in the
garden—except the tree of the knowledge of good and evil. If you
eat its fruit, you are sure to die."

But when Satan contradicted God's Word, Adam stood silent.
The Bible says he was with Eve (Gen. 3:6), which means he could
have corrected the devil's false information. But he didn't do that.
He let Eve respond to the serpent, and her replay of God's instructions was wrong. She added to what God had said by telling the serpent that they were not even to touch the fruit of the tree (Gen. 3:3).
God had simply told them not to eat of it.

When Satan directly challenged God's command, he did not
experience any opposition. So he kept going. He could see that
Adam and Eve were open to deception; one did not know God's
word well, and the other stood silent when it was contradicted. So
Satan introduced them to another way of eternal life. He fed them
the lie that if they ate of the tree, they would not die but would be
exposed to knowledge God had been trying to keep secret. They
would know good and evil (as if knowing good and evil is a good
thing), and this would make them like God.

Why would God allow Adam and Eve to go through this temptation? Because He wanted them to choose who would be lord of their
lives. The woman was convinced when she saw the beauty of the
tree and how delicious its fruit looked that she wanted the wisdom
it would give her. She was convinced that the tree would give her
something God would not.

The lie of the occult is that the wisdom that comes from hidden knowledge will give us what we desire. But the Bible tells us in 1 John 2:16: "For everything in the world—the cravings of sinful man, the lust of his eyes, and the boasting of what he has and does—comes not from the Father but from the world." What the world has to offer will only fulfill the lust of the eyes, the lust of the flesh, and the pride of life. But God will generously provide *all* that we need.

When Adam and Eve ate of the forbidden tree, their eyes were indeed opened—to what they had done. They had fallen for a lie, experienced evil, and now were mired in shame.

Reaching Out

The lie the serpent spouted in the garden is still wreaking havoc today. People continue to fall for the deception that there is truth outside of God, and they continue to reap the same shame and torment that plagued Adam and Eve. Thankfully there is an answer— the love of Jesus. His death repaired the breach created in the garden and allowed us to again experience the joy of knowing God intimately.

Believe it or not, this kind of love relationship is exactly what occultists are seeking, and it is my prayer that you will allow the Holy Spirit to use you to reach out to them. No matter what form of occultism people practice, the way to reach them is to show them the love of Christ. This will enable them to "see" the truth about Christianity—that it is not a religious exercise but a relationship with a loving God who will never leave them or forsake them. He will be their provider and transform them into His likeness. This is exactly what every occultist is looking for.

Working hand in hand with showing occultists love is our witness as followers of Christ. The way we live before them every day will serve as proof of the truth of Jesus Christ. As members of the body of Christ we are His witnesses. Every day our words and actions testify of God's presence in the world. This is why it is vital that people see Jesus living in us. They must see the true character of Christ reflected in our lifestyle. Philippians 1:11 says, "May you always be filled with the fruit of your salvation—the righteous character produced in your life by Jesus Christ—for this will bring much glory and praise to God" (NLT).

Many people think they have to go out of their way to encounter an occult follower. The truth is, we probably encounter someone who is or has been involved in the occult each day among the dozens of people we interact with. Remember, someone who simply reads his horoscope for direction is as much a practicing occultist as a self-proclaimed witch. His religion is astrology, and he practices it by reading the horoscope.

Of course, you may not know exactly who is and who isn't relying on the stars for direction in life. That is why the character you reveal is so important. If an occultist is tired of the torment in his life and wants to find another way, your witness will help him determine whether you are genuine, trustworthy, and safe enough to open up to.

Because how you live when you think no one is watching is so vital to ministering to those in the occult (and anyone else for that matter), I encourage you to think about these questions. Do the people in your daily life see you as approachable, humble, and authentic? Are you the type of Christian others desire to be around? There are some people who make you happy when they arrive, and there are some who make you happy when they leave. Which are you? A Christian's actions speak louder than his words ever will.

The term "to minister" means to give attendance or aid, to provide for someone's wants or needs. Ministering to occultists can mean providing for their needs, being a listening ear, or just giving them a hug if they need it. If they have a problem, we can offer to pray for them. Believe it or not, most will appreciate the offer, because it shows we are concerned.

Reaching occultists isn't as difficult as you may have been taught to believe. After all, they are just people with needs and desires much like yours. Just keep the following things in mind as you reach out to them.

Connect.

Connecting with someone who truly cares is a basic human need. Those involved in or coming out of the occult have a vacuum in their heart that they've been trying to fill through occultism. They may be dealing with hurt, anger, or past abuse, and God may want to use you to help them find healing in Him. Most of the time occultists want to fully reveal themselves to someone. They want to share exactly who they are. Having godly character and showing you genuinely care will help them trust that you are safe. As they open up to you, listen and do not try to fix them. Then offer counsel from God's Word. It addresses every condition of man's heart and contains the truth that will set them free.

Know the truth.

Obviously the occultist is in need of the truth, so it is imperative for Christians to know who God is and what His Word says. This may sound surprisingly simple, but I have encountered many former occultists who have ended up confused because the Christians who wanted to help them did not know God or understand His Word. They had devised doctrines that were not supported in Scripture.

Walk in the power of the Holy Spirit.

The person who ministers to the occultist needs to be filled with the Holy Spirit. By this I mean he or she needs to be someone who reflects God's character, practices only what the Bible teaches, and speaks the truth in love. Once the occultist begins to hear the truth and see Christ in the Christian, either his heart will soften and he will become open to receiving Jesus as his Savior, or he will walk away. There is a real tendency for Christians to want to do more than is necessary. Allow the Holy Spirit to work in the occultist's life. You are to reflect Christ's character. That will be your witness.

Pray.

I cannot express strongly enough how essential prayer is. You must pray for the occultist to make the decision to walk in truth so he or she will become a disciple of Christ and be set free. The Bible says, "You are truly my disciples if you remain faithful to my teachings. And you will know the truth, and the truth will set you free" (John 8:31–32, NLT).

Do not become impatient with the process. Occultists will come to Christ only because the Holy Spirit worked in their life and drew them to Himself. Our involvement becomes interference when we put God or the occultist on our timetable. We must let God be God.

The above list is by no means exhaustive. I am simply starting a discussion that all the authors in this book will contribute to. The stories you are about to read will give you insight into who these former occultists used to be, what they practiced, how Jesus met them where they were, and how they found true freedom in Christ. I pray that their testimonies will not only open a window for you into the mind-set of the occultist but also prick your heart with love and compassion for them.

Chapter 1

FROM DEMON HABITATION TO TEMPLE OF THE HOLY SPIRIT

By Jeff Harshbarger

MUNCIE, INDIANA. 1981.
"You're angelically oppressed." The man I considered my spiritual teacher kept his gaze from meeting mine. His low voice made me think he might not want the others to hear. This man had been my mentor. I had modeled my life after him. I had given him power over me, and I obeyed his commands. He had all the answers, and this was all he could say? *What!?*

For the last four years I had been a practicing Satanist. I had given myself completely to my lord Lucifer. He, or at least his demons, had taken up residence in me. I had experienced their presence and their power. Yet somehow that autumn, while studying to be a child psychologist at Ball State University, I experienced something new. I felt, at least spiritually, what seemed to be an impenetrable wall in front of me.

This wall completely locked me out of the demonic life I pursued. It seemed no ritual or ceremony could reconnect me with my demonic masters; I felt dry and brittle. I could watch but not truly participate in the practice of my coven. As a result I became painfully detached from what had fed me for the last four years. Depression seeped into my soul like a cold, wet fog. How I hated it. How I longed to find an answer.

My mentor's explanation made my blood boil. To think the

person who introduced me to Satan was telling me that God-serving angels stood in the way of my spiritual pursuits. I flew into a rage. I determined that this God had no real power (or so I thought). So I planned to throw myself more completely into my devotion to Lucifer.

I did everything I knew to do. I mustered every ounce of rebellion toward God I felt in my heart. I set out to be as destructive as I could toward anyone or anything that crossed me. I called upon the demonic in ways I had not practiced in the previous four years.

Up to this point in my life as a Satanist I had been an angel of light. I cared about the younger members of our coven and listened to their problems. I did not hurt anyone but simply manipulated the weak to do my bidding. Now I wanted nothing more than to work the "nice guy" out of me. Why should I care about anyone? I figured it was time for my coven members to take care of themselves.

My only desire was to do the bidding of the demons inside me and crucify my human heart. A good way to do that would be to curse people just for the fun of it, so that is what I did. I would pick a random person, pronounce a curse upon him, and send a demon or two after him.

I went on walks and actively prayed to demons, giving them my heart's desire in hopes that my own longings would die. My greatest desire was to find a lifelong companion who loved me unconditionally. I wanted a wife and a family. But even this I was willing to sacrifice to show my commitment to my master. And still the wall continued to stand in the way.

How could this be? How could this God of the Bible, this weak Jesus whom my master had killed, be able to stop Satan? The thought hit me like a sledgehammer one afternoon. I walked along the Muncie River trying unsuccessfully to focus on demonic prayer. The question had power. I tried to shove it away, but the evidence stood out like the awful neon clothing so popular at the time. I could not ignore it.

Then the inevitable happened. Because the demons inside me

could not torment others through me, they took pleasure in tormenting me instead. I could not sleep, food tasted terrible, and finding a quiet place to be alone became utterly impossible. This is what it had come down to: I had served Satan faithfully, and in my hour of need he made me his enemy.

You would think at this point that a sane person would simply close the door and walk away. Why serve someone, something, anything so bent on making a person miserable, especially when a more powerful God exists?

We humans are funny creatures. We've chosen allegiance with Satan over relationship with God since the Garden of Eden. We are self-destructive. We'd rather cheat on a test than study, speed to work than leave home on time. We don't want anyone to tell us what to do. It boils down to pride. *I can make my own choices—I can, I can, I can.* And that is exactly how I thought.

I was so completely engrossed in my lifestyle that I failed to see the practical. I had sworn to never serve Jesus, and I would keep my word. So I decided that I would have to die.

This would be a great convenience to my coven because we had just started contemplating the idea of human sacrifice. Who better than me? Not only would I help the coven reach the next level of satanic intimacy, but I would also be a martyr, a hero. The thought so inflated my ego that I became excited. Surely Satan himself would welcome me into hell.

I would be the ultimate Satanist. Nothing would stop me now. Except Steve, my spiritual teacher, who said, "No."

Never in my life had I suffered such a slap in the face. I wasn't good enough? They did not want me to die an honorable death? We'd see about that.

Not even three weeks later I sat on a bed in a local hotel. I took a drag from the joint in my fingers then gulped whiskey straight from the bottle. What a way to go—numb, drunk, and depressed. All I would have to do is put the gun to my head and pull the trigger. So I put the barrel against my head. The cold, rough steel bit into my temple.

Was I afraid? No, even though I knew I should have been. I tightened my fingers around the trigger and took a deep breath.

Suddenly a thought floated through my mind that I had not expected. It took me by surprise: *Where are you going to spend eternity?* Could I be going mad? Why would a Satanist care where he spent eternity? He would know: hell is the only choice.

Then, for the first time, the cold hand of fear *did* grip my heart. Maybe I did not want to go to hell after all. My hands shook, and I placed the gun back on the bed. I stared at it for the longest time as my mind drifted through the events that had led me to this place. My eyelids grew heavy, and I fell into a restless sleep until sunlight seeped between the heavy drapes.

The Presence in the Backyard

The next morning I headed home, if you could call it that. The house I shared with Steve and a few coven members served more as a place to party and conduct rituals than an actual place to live. I walked into an empty house that reeked of stale beer and cigarettes, my roommates already gone for the day to work or school. The effects of last night's drug-induced stupor had completely evaporated. My mind felt clear.

The silence angered me as I considered the fact that I had lived through the night. I shouldn't even be here. I should be dead. How ridiculous it seemed that fear got the best of me last night. Well, this time I would not fail. And I would do this thing *now*.

I went to the garage, found a good length of rope, and made a noose. Next, a chair. The old wooden one in the corner would do. I placed it under the rafter and tossed the rope up and over. After I double-checked to make sure it held, I slipped the noose over my head. The needlelike cords scratched my neck, but I didn't care. I did not count to three; I did not allow myself to weasel out this time. I kicked the chair out from under me.

I felt a sharp jerk on my neck and then searing pain as the hard ground knocked the wind out of my chest. Somehow the rope had come untied, and I landed on the floor. Misery washed over me like a tidal wave. I stumbled back into the house, sat in a chair, and waited the day out.

One by one the members of my coven returned—Steve with a case of beer, another with plenty of dope. Apparently my teacher wanted to party. I popped open a beer and brought it to my face. Just the smell of if made my stomach flip. No way would I drink that. I put it down.

I rolled a joint and placed it to my lips. The thing made my mouth burn. I couldn't even party! I crushed the nasty thing in an ashtray and saw that Steve was watching me. I glared at him and turned my back.

"Let's take this party somewhere else." Steve grabbed the case of beer and headed out the door. Guess he didn't want the younger members to see just how well Satanism was working for his second-in-command.

After they left, nothing was left but silence, and a crushing misery gripped my heart. I sank onto my bed and hugged my pillow. I could not eat. I could not sleep. I took no pleasure in life. I could not even die. I was a complete and total failure. Maybe I had been doomed to live a life of total pain.

A sob wracked my body, and the next thing I knew I could not stop crying. I cried tears from deep in my heart, tears I had never shed—for my broken family, my lonely life, my wretched existence.

Then from the foot of my bed a voice came from nowhere: "Get out." I froze. Maybe Satan had sent a demon to kill me for my failure to end my life. I watched and waited. Then from right beside my face, the bodiless voice spoke again: "Get out!"

Goose bumps prickled my arms. The command could not be any clearer. Immediately I rolled off the bed, slid the old wooden window up, and stepped out to my backyard and into the presence of the God I had run from for so long. I fell on my face.

I felt God's presence so strong I did not need to ask who stood before me. I knew. And in that moment, on my face in the back-yard, I made the choice I should have made all along. "Jesus," I prayed, "just make my life OK."

I'll never know just how long I stayed there in the backyard, but when I went back inside, I knew I had changed. I crawled into bed and slept peacefully all night.

The next morning I slowly opened my eyes. Not yet ready to get out of bed, I thought about the last night's incredible experience. Had it all been a dream? Maybe a figment of my imagination?

I sat up slowly. The memory of the voice reverberated in my head. Then I remembered the amazing, awesome presence in my back-yard, and I realized how profoundly peaceful my heart felt. Then I realized that I had slept the whole night through. Amazing.

The thump from the front door as it closed drew my attention. Steve had come home. He shuffled through the house and into the kitchen. I rose from my bed, still in the same clothes I had worn the night before. How amazingly detached I felt. I had definitely changed. Throughout the day as more coven members came home, I felt it more and more. I no longer belonged.

So I withdrew. Walking away from a satanic coven is not an easy thing to do, but I knew I had to. Instead of partying, I studied. Instead of performing rituals, I went on walks. This went on for about a week.

One afternoon I escaped to the basement to work on laundry. I thought, like all the days before, that Steve would eventually leave the house to get away from the new me. The creak of the old base-ment steps told me I was wrong. He had come to join me but not to help me fold my blue jeans.

"What's up with you?" The fire in his eyes betrayed him. He already knew the answer.

"What do you mean?" I had to be careful. The man had a temper.

"You're just not the same." He looked down at me as I sat folding clothes and crossed his arms. "You haven't done a thing with us all week. No rituals, no parties. Why?"

I stood up then and looked him straight in the eye. "I haven't wanted to."

"You've pulled away." Steve took a step toward me. I could feel his question before he asked it. "What god do you serve?"

This was it. The encounter I had was far too real to lie about it. I stood my ground and kept my eyes focused on his.

"Not yours," I said.

Steve punched me on the jaw so hard I flew across the laundry room and landed on my back. I expected more, but he only glared at me, eyes blazing, and then stormed up the stairs.

Is that all he's got? I rubbed my throbbing jaw and stood. My whole body ached, but the realization that hit me gave me strength. My mentor had just lost his power over me.

A few days later Steve and my coven members moved out! Why, I'm not exactly sure, but they left me to live there in that house all by myself. What a relief. Now I could devote myself to becoming reacquainted with this God who had so changed me.

QUICK FACTS ABOUT SATANISM

• Satan is the archenemy of almighty God; he is the leader of the fallen angels—a created being whose power can never equal the power of God.

• Satan is not a god: he is neither omniscient (knowing all things) nor omnipresent (everywhere at once).

• It is impossible for Satan or his demons to read minds; they cannot know the secret thoughts of human beings.

• Satanists are divided into two main categories: traditionalists, who believe Satan is a unique spirit being, and modernists, who define all evil generally as Satan.

• Jesus Christ directly challenged and defeated Satan's power and authority during His earthly ministry; Christians need not fear Satan or Satanists, since the Holy Spirit resides within them.[1]

A Date With Freedom

Where should I begin? Church maybe? The Christians I knew all went to church, so I decided that is where I would start. But I certainly didn't think of myself as a Christian. I wasn't really sure *what* to call myself. I knew I no longer served Satan, and I had no doubt about my encounter with Jesus in the backyard. But if at this period of my life someone had asked me whom I served, I would probably have said I didn't know.

The first church I visited stood not all that far from my home. To me large churches were stuffy and uninviting, but I needed help, so I determined to go. It made sense to go somewhere close to home; this way if church was as boring and awful as I remembered, I could get out of there fast and be home in no time.

I chose a Wednesday night service to make my entrance. I sat in the back on a cushioned pew next to several elderly saints. I waited through a sermon and a choir song before anyone greeted me. Finally I was introduced to the pastor.

Before I go any further, I would like to point out that, like me, many occultists seeking help want to find someone who will meet them where they are. I stood before the pastor demon-possessed, suicidal, and crying out for help, but he did not seem interested in my personal life at all. He seemed more concerned that I knew about the church's various programs and the building project. It felt as though I stood in the showroom of a car dealership, and the pastor was showing me all of the church's bells and whistles. I didn't need an ice cream social in the new gym. I needed someone to hear me.

I left as soon as I could get away. I thought if this church did not cut the mustard, then maybe another one would. Muncie had lots of churches. Over the next several weeks I went from church to church. I learned a lot—about Sunday school classes and service times and how the music ministry could really usher in the Spirit, not that I knew what *that* meant.

The oddest thing seemed to be that during my years as a Satanist I had been pursued by a lot of Christians. They told me that Jesus loved me and had a plan for my life, and that they were praying for me. Yet now that I had met Jesus, I couldn't find a Christian who would take the time to listen to me. That all changed when I met Harry and Jo Richardson.

On a Wednesday evening I crept into a small church. I thought I could hide in the back and listen to the sermon without being noticed, but the place was so tiny even the back pew felt like the front. Four or five people smiled and waved to me from their seats. I nodded in return, resisting the urge to flee. This place felt different, so different in fact that the demons inside me became *very* agitated. They wanted me out of that church, and I knew it. I gripped the pew and held on, feeling extremely uncomfortable.

When the service ended, I stuck around, as I had many times before, to see if I could find help. A man who sported a corduroy blazer and blue jeans approached me. He had a round face with kind eyes and a head that used to hold brown hair but was now bald except for what was left growing around the bottom.

"I'm Harry Richardson." The man stuck out his hand. His Boston accent made him sound very intelligent. "My wife, Jo, and I would like to invite you to dinner this Friday."

"Jeff Harshbarger." I shook the hand he held out to me, but I wasn't sure I had heard him correctly. "You want me to come for dinner?"

A woman with snowy white hair piled high into a fluffy bun came to Harry's side and smiled at me. "I'm Jo. Just tell us where you live, and we'll pick you up." Car service and a free meal? Who could turn that down?

October can be cold in Indiana. The sun sets early, taking with it any semblance of warmth. Friday night I waited in my house wondering if this couple would actually show. Every now and then I peeked out into the cold, dark street. I could feel a frigid draft seep through the old wooden window. It would probably frost tonight.

I looked at my watch; six o'clock, and the sun had disappeared already. Maybe they had other things to do. I could hear evil thoughts inside me: *They don't really care. You're still all alone.* Just minutes after those words floated through my mind, headlights rounded the corner, and a silver Reliant K (Remember those cars? So boxy and so conservative) stopped where the sidewalk connected my front door to the street. Jo and Harry had come!

I rode in the backseat enveloped in an awkward silence. I saw the streetlights, green and red, reflected through Harry's glasses. We made a turn down a street in the kind of neighborhood I saw only on television. It had beautiful houses and sprawling lawns with huge trees. *These people lived here?* I looked at my faded blue jeans and flannel shirt and then out the window to the prettiest home on the block.

The house was a large two-story graystone with a green roof and a green front door. Welcoming lights sparkled through the shuttered windows, and I could make out lace curtains on the second floor. Compared to my upbringing, it seemed as though I had just been invited to dinner with the Kennedys.

An incredible peace greeted me inside the house. I thought at first that it came from the beautiful but homey décor—white carpet, French wallpaper, and a white stone fireplace. Or maybe it was the aroma of dinner wafting from the kitchen. But the longer I stayed, the more I felt certain this peace came not from my surroundings but from the Spirit living in the house.

Dinner could not have been more delicious. I had never had ham loaf before, but from the first taste I was hooked. Jo proceeded to ply me with food until I thought I would explode. She had such a warm and engaging personality that I soon forgot I was dining in the home of a Ball State professor and her husband, the head librarian. I felt more like I was in the home of two close friends. A part of my heart wished I could just stay with them and be their son.

Unfortunately, the demons inside me did *not* like the Richardsons.

"Are you from around here? Where did you grow up? What's your major?" Jo and Harry's gentle inquiries into my personal life made them very angry. I began to doubt. What should I disclose? Should I lie about my satanic past? That would be easy. At this point lying would be the normal thing to do.

Then a new thought entered my mind. What if I trusted them? Would that make me vulnerable and weak? I made up my mind to wait until after dinner to make my decision.

We moved to the living room. I sat on a long green couch; Jo and Harry sat in upholstered chairs. I knew I would have to trust them. So I told them of my college career and my interest in psychology.

"And what about God? Do you know Him?" Jo seemed so dainty at first, but as she leaned forward, as if not wanting to miss a word, I felt a strength in her that surprised me. Harry lifted his eyebrows. Apparently he was looking for an answer as well.

I pulled at my thumb. This would be harder than I thought. "Um, that's why I came to your church. For the past four years I've been a practicing Satanist." I shrugged. "I thought maybe someone could help me."

The understanding that flashed across Jo's eyes was lightening quick. She smiled, stood, and walked to where I was seated. She took me by the hand, and I had no choice but to stand. At the same time she held her hand out to Harry and said, "Harry, we need to pray."

With the three of us standing together in the living room, Jo Richardson called upon the name of Jesus. She prayed with her eyes closed, and the demons inside me were now so full of rage they began to take over my body. I could feel them rise up inside me, physically turn my head, and glare at her. At the same moment Jo's eyes opened. She lifted her head, and when she looked back, I saw the strength of God, and I felt the absolute terror of the beings that lived inside me.

"Come out of him in the name of Jesus." Her steady voice and confidence said she expected the demons to obey. And they did.

Just like that. No puking, no writhing on the floor, no Hollywood moments—the demons just left. And that was it. I was free. How funny that I had spent four years trying to fill myself with as many of the strongest demons I could, and the simple prayer of a white-haired lady would be enough to send them all packing.

I felt as though shutters snapped open inside my soul, and light began to pour in. "I need a mirror!" I began to run because I felt so free.

"Down the hall, first door on the right!" Jo turned me by the shoulders.

I took off in the direction she pointed, found the bathroom, and flipped the light on. I looked at my face; it looked different. Then I looked into my eyes, and for the first time in four years I saw *me* instead of them.

"They're gone!" I shouted, not knowing if I should laugh or cry. I ran back into the living room not bothering to turn off the bathroom light.

"I know!" Jo grinned and hugged me like I belonged to her. We all laughed and danced and thanked Jesus for the next few hours. I smiled so hard my face began to hurt, and Jo thought that was really funny. She grabbed my hand. "Now you need to be born again." Jo pulled me over to where Harry stood.

"What does that mean?" I had heard the expression, and now, finally, I received an explanation. Jo and Harry explained the gospel—that I needed to repent of my sin, and they told me exactly what that meant. Now I knew I needed to stop doing things I had always done, such as lying. They told me I needed to give Jesus my life, that I should submit to Him and make Him my Lord and Savior. And that cold October night in Jo and Harry's living room, with a tummy full of ham loaf, I was set free and became a child of God.

During the next few days I found myself truly living in a whole new world. With the eyes of my heart open, I began to experience

2 Corinthians 5:17: "Therefore, if anyone is in Christ, he is a new creation; the old is gone, the new has come!"

As though I had been raised from a dark dream to a majestic sunrise, my senses came alive and my mind seemed crystal clear. I found myself thinking constantly about this God who had interrupted my life, who had saved me from my own destruction. For the first time I knew love. I took long walks just to be alone with Him because for the first time I was in love—with Jesus. I found myself amazed at the beauty of His creation. I saw that "the heavens declare the glory of God; the skies proclaim the work of his hands" (Ps. 19:1).

Like a man raised from the dead, I could truly see creation. While looking at a simple tree, I saw His handiwork. I once looked at the sky and saw the sun shooting brilliant rays of gold from behind a silver cloud, and the evidence of God's glory overwhelmed me. I looked at my feet and saw a single yellow flower growing from a rock, and its beauty made me cry. I was entirely new. I was free. I had no demons inside me. I had a God who loved me, and I loved Him because He did. I had assurance that He would never leave me or forsake me (Heb. 13:5).

NEW LIFE IN CHRIST

Once on one of my frequent walks I stumbled upon a Christian bookstore. I knew I needed a Bible, so I went inside. What a surprise.

This store had every kind of Christian anything a person could dream of. Wall art and candles embossed with scriptures, T-shirts and dress ties, socks and shoelaces. Books—so many books about anything pertaining to the Bible that I couldn't count them all. And Jesus...stuff. I didn't know what else to call it: pencils and note paper and little erasers and bumper stickers about not being perfect, just forgiven. The whole place smelled like a little old lady's parlor, which I later learned was "Fruit of the Spirit" potpourri.

I nearly turned right around to leave, but I saw a big sign that said "Bibles." I made a determined dash to the bookshelf under the sign. I had no idea just how many different Bibles were available. I took one look and gave up. I left the store very confused.

Back to Harry and Jo I went. They talked with the pastor of the church I now attended on a regular basis, and he made sure that someone gave me a Bible. It was a beautiful onion-skinned King James Version. Now I've read the King James Bible from cover to cover and use it frequently. But at the time, like most messed-up twenty-one-year-olds, I couldn't make heads or tails of it. I read it anyway because I knew Christians should read the Bible, but I understood only bits and pieces. Then I remembered someone at church who said something about a Bible in normal language. *That* was exactly what I needed.

So I made a second trip to the Bible bookstore. I decided to do the sensible thing and ask a clerk to help me find the right version. And for Christmas that year I received a brand-new *Living Bible*. It met me where I was and enabled me to understand God's Word, which to a former occultist is vitally important, second only to salvation itself.

How different my life had become. In just a matter of a few months I had gone from being a suicidal, demon-possessed Satanist (who in reality was just a lost child looking for love, family, and a reason to live) to someone found by, protected by, and provided for by God.

He took me to the right church when I sought help. He sent to me the right couple, Jo and Harry, who took the time to listen to and to pray for me. Not only did they invite me into their home, but also they invited me into their lives. And through the acceptance of this retired couple, sent by God, I became His child. And Harry and Jo became my family. But most importantly, because of them I realized that God loved me. My greatest need had been filled. Now the process of re-parenting, as Jo used to call it, could begin.

After I was born again, Jo and Harry insisted that I needed to fellowship with Christians, among other things. "You do not need to fly solo," Jo would say. "If you need a ride just tell us. Even if you're halfway across town, we'll come and get you."

They did quite frequently. One night after service Harry, again wearing his blue jeans and corduroy blazer, walked over to me from across the church. "I would like to invite you to a Full Gospel Business Men's meeting." His formal manner seemed almost comical.

"*Businessmen?* Why would I go to a meeting of businessmen?" I pictured a group of older men all dressed in pinstriped suits. What would a former Satanist want with a bunch of swells? I felt uncomfortable already.

"It's not what you think." Harry shook his head. "We don't talk business. We talk about Jesus."

"There's always a really good dinner too," Jo chimed in from two pews away. "You'll be our guest." She always knew where to hit me: my stomach.

"Sounds good then." I tried not to let them see my delight at the prospect of another free meal.

Once more I got to ride in the Reliant K. Sometimes I still marveled at the probability of such an odd pairing—the art professor, the head librarian, and the former Satanist. Who else but God would strike such a friendship?

I followed Jo and Harry into the Ball State student conference center. Outside of a plate of baked chicken and chocolate pudding for dessert, I had no idea what this meeting had in store for me.

The dining room would have been enough to make me very uncomfortable if it had not been for my two companions. The tables held beautiful china and linen tablecloths. People dressed nicely and spoke in quiet tones.

It's funny that after all the years of serving Satan and never having anything, only two months after giving my life to Christ I would find myself at a fine dinner with the kind of people I used to dream of having around me. My first encounter with a group of Christians outside of church turned out to be a positive one. These people accepted me right away, and any anxiety I had about not fitting in just evaporated.

We sat at a table full of pleasant people: Jo and Harry, of course, and a guy named Rick, who had been a Christian about as long as I had. He could not contain his excitement at his newfound faith. After dessert had been served and the dishes taken away, the meeting began.

The guest speaker came to share his testimony. I don't remember the guy's name, but he was a tall, skinny preacher with a whole lot of energy. I watched wide-eyed as he moved across the stage, Bible in hand. He began to share that Jesus Christ had not only come into his life as Lord and Savior, but now he was filled with the Holy Spirit.

What on earth did that mean? I tried to remember what I'd read from the Book of Matthew, the only part of the Bible I had read so far. And the King James Version read like a Shakespeare play. Did I understand what I'd read? Not really. Even still I did not remember reading anything about a Holy Spirit.

I turned to Jo and whispered, "Holy Spirit? I know about Jesus. Are there two of them?"

"Shh, just listen." Jo pointed to the speaker and smiled. What had I said that was so funny?

But the preacher went on to share how the Holy Spirit would come inside and fill the Christian, and that He would enable the Christian to live a godly life. I wanted nothing more than to know God more and to be filled with His Spirit as I had been filled with the demonic. I had known the ugliness of life with an unholy spirit. How much better it would be to be full of the Holy Spirit instead. Yep. That's what I wanted.

The preacher said that if anyone wanted to be filled with the Holy Spirit, he should come forward to receive prayer. Yikes! Right now? In front of all these people? I looked to Harry and Jo. "Do I go up there?"

"*Yes!*" Jo gave an emphatic nod and nearly pushed me out of my chair. I looked down and saw my feet moving. I looked up, and the preacher was coming at me speaking a language I didn't understand. He laid his hand on my forehead, and I experienced a warm, electric sensation, almost like water being filled in a cup, that seemed to course from my toes to my head. My knees buckled, and I found myself on the floor swimming in what I can only describe as an ocean of love.

Before I knew it, someone grabbed me by the hand and helped me to my feet. And a language came out of my mouth that I did not understand. What a shock. Nothing this good ever happened when I served the devil. God sure is full of surprises. I thought all I was going to get was a plate of food.

Up to that point I had experienced God through external things—meeting Him in my backyard, finding Harry and Jo. Being filled with the Holy Spirit allowed me to know God on the inside of me. I could feel His presence just as I had felt the demons, but He never possessed me. God loved me.

Christmas meant so much that year. I received my new *Living Bible*, and suddenly the Word of God became vibrant and alive. Until then the Bible had been the book Christians read, something written a thousand years ago and very hard to understand. Now I not only understood everything I read, but I also could not put the book down.

And God began to teach me through His Word. Hebrews 13:5 became His first promise to me: "For God has said, 'I will never fail you. I will never abandon you'" (NLT). Now I had the understanding. And with His first promise to my heart, I now knew that this mighty God would not abandon this once-lost child because He told me so.

THE WARFARE BEGINS

That time in my life was like a honeymoon period for me. Everything was new, God was real, I reconnected with my family, and I began to carve out a new life as a child of God. The first thing I needed to be a productive child of God was a job. So one day in late August, just before the students returned to Ball State, I walked into a small but popular eatery and put in an application. The owner hired me on the spot. I asked if I could start that day, and he said, "You bet."

Man, did I have fun at that job. I became a sandwich builder/delivery guy. I used to stack boxed sandwiches in the back of my tiny silver Toyota until the Styrofoam boxes touched the roof. I earned enough money in tips alone to pay my rent.

Rent was easy too. I moved into a beautiful house near the campus. This was a home specifically for Christian bachelors. Who lived there already? Rick, the guy I sat next to at the Full Gospel Business Men's meeting. A coincidence? Not really. New life, new job, new place to live, new child of God—I thought all my problems were over. How wrong I was.

This is when the warfare began. My old companions, the demons I had known for years, showed up. I had not yet read the scripture that said they *would* come back.

> When an evil spirit comes out of a man, it goes through arid places seeking rest and does not find it. Then it says, "I will return to the house I left." When it arrives, it finds the house unoccupied, swept clean and put in order. Then it goes and takes with it seven other spirits more wicked than itself, and they go in and live there. And the final condition of that man is worse than the first.
>
> —Matthew 12:43–45

That's exactly what they did. The demons came back sevenfold to see if I was serious about serving Jesus. Their intent: to repossess and to destroy me. Nothing could have perplexed me more. Why would this happen? Hadn't I given my life to Christ? Most importantly, why would God, who loved me, allow this to occur? Familiar anger began to simmer in my heart.

I had no idea my former anger toward God had not been automatically taken out of my heart. I still had to deal with it. That anger was the reason I became a Satanist in the first place. My old companions knew it. The demons tried to make me angry with God again so they could repossess me.

I went to Harry and Jo about the demonic attack, but I did not tell them of my feelings toward God. The anger in my heart bore fruit. I hid from the people closest to me. I did not realize that if I could not be honest, Jo and Harry could not help me.

Jo explained to me through Scripture the reality of spiritual warfare to a Christian. What she said only angered me more. I thought I should be exempt, that I would never experience a demonic presence again. What pride!

Now, looking back, I know God had orchestrated the whole thing. He allowed the demons to attack so I would finally deal with the anger in my heart. But at the time the demonic presence offended me. Somehow I had swallowed the lie that because I was now a Christian, the lonely days of suffering had ended. I did not realize that God would use the demonic to trigger my deepest issue—but for His purpose.

I was angry. Of course, I was. I had lived my whole life in anger; what else did I know? The difference now was that though I seethed at God, He still lived inside me. This time I chose correctly. My first choice, and I know this to be the work of the Holy Spirit, was that I refused to give myself over to the demons that triggered my anger. I had tasted and seen the goodness of the Lord, and I knew the dregs of life with my old companions. Who in their right mind would return to that?

Still, I harbored anger toward God for allowing the demons access to me. I did not understand why a loving God would let these things torment me so. I found my circumstance inexcusable. Having nowhere else to go, I returned to Harry and Jo to find a solution.

I explained the anger I was feeling despite what Jo had told me about spiritual warfare, and we talked about the situation. Jo said, "You're a child of God in the middle of spiritual warfare, something we all face in one form or another. It's something God uses to mold us into His image. God is faithful. You're not your own; you were bought with a price. It seems to me that you want God to be who *you* want Him to be instead of who He really is. You want life on your terms, not on His."

She was right. Did the woman always have to be right? Jo kept talking in her matter-of-fact manner. "In fact, God is in such control that in reality the demons no longer have power over you. All you need to do is to submit to God, His Spirit, and His Word. Submit to God, resist the devil, and he will flee." (See James 4:7.)

"But I'm so angry. I can't stop being angry." I thought that maybe if I said it again, my burning rage would be validated.

"You need to give it to God." Jo's intense gray eyes held my attention.

"Give God my anger? I can't give God my anger. It's ugly."

"But even our righteousness is a filthy rag to God. All we have to give Him is our sin. The best we can do is not to hide it like Adam tried to."

And Jo once more hit the nail on the head, as she would do so many times. Showing me how to relate to God as a sinner saved by His grace taught me again that through good or bad times I needed to be faithful to the One who was faithful to me. This time Jo didn't pray for me; she made *me* pray. I prayed in repentance, confessed my anger, and gave it to Him. I told the Lord I would embrace whatever He brought into my life.

If Jesus Christ would be Lord of my life, then whatever came my way was something He allowed. I learned, as Romans 8:28 says, "that God causes everything to work together for the good of those who love God and are called to his purpose for them" (NLT). Even if that meant persevering through the demonic.

If God wanted to test my heart, He could. Did I really love Him for who He is, or did I love Him for what He could do for me? If

I suffered, would I be tempted as Job was tempted by his wife to curse God and die? (See Job 2:9.) Or would I submit to His purpose and be conformed to His image? The sanctifying work of the Holy Spirit had begun. Again, by His mercy, I chose the right thing.

I loved God. How could I make one who was so good out to be bad? I chose to not curse God and die. I chose to accept God as He is, not create a false image reflecting who I wanted Him to be. For the rest of my life I would give myself over to the Holy Spirit so He would make me a true disciple of Christ. Jesus promised that He would never leave me or forsake me. How could I possibly forsake Him? I could not.

And with that decision the demonic presence that tormented me so began to go away. It did not have a place in me. God answered the cry of my heart. He was still giving heed to the simple prayer I prayed that desperate night in my backyard. I asked that He make everything OK, and He did.

God Is Bigger

I learned and am still learning to rely on the everlasting presence of God—the One who saved me, the One I call my Lord, the One who baptized and filled me with His Spirit. God said He would never leave me or forsake me. In all these years He never has, and His presence has completely disarmed the demonic (Col. 2:15).

If I could say any one thing to believers and nonbelievers alike, it would be that God is simply bigger. He is bigger than Satan and his demons, and there is no power on earth or in heaven greater. In His sovereignty God overshadowed the darkness that hung over me. He took away the power of the devil.

No matter what happens, no matter how awful, God is simply bigger. We are bought with a price. What will God allow to happen in order to draw you to Him? In the midst of my struggle, I learned to trust Him enough to say, "Though He slay me, yet will I trust Him" (Job 13:15, NKJV). It took a painful season of warfare for me to realize that God is in control no matter what. The reality of God's presence, of His sovereign will, is the fact that He works all things together for the good of those who love Him. I came to see that He was working in me for His purpose all along.

God is who He says He is. And when that truth finally sank into my heart, the power that compelled me to live in fear, the very thing that caused me to react in anger to the warfare I encountered, was unplugged. I saw in my heart a true transformation begin. I saw that to live an abundant life meant to be controlled by the Holy Spirit. He taught me, and I'm still learning, to stand in the power of His might. I know that for the rest of my days as a Christian, God will keep me and that He will walk with me. As I submit to Him, the devil will flee. It's as simple as that. I now know in my heart to stand and resist. I know that God is my refuge and strength.

Knowing this, my question to the body of Christ is, Why are we so afraid? There are books and more books on everything demonic—how to break their power, how to overcome what they do to us. Yet we seem to forget that God has twice as many angels as there are demons. That's a great majority. We forget that in sheer numbers there are more angels at work in men's lives than there are demons. My life is an example of that.

I was a Satanist who was oppressed by the angelic. Oppression is simply a spirit, be it angelic or demonic, trying to work in a person's life. Angels worked on me; they stopped the demons in their tracks. The effect brought me to the Lord Jesus Christ.

How should a Christian deal with demonic oppression? By not allowing it to send him into a tailspin. If you are a Christian, you've been bought with a price; you're not your own. You've been filled with His Spirit, and God stands ready to help you. (See Hebrews 4:16.)

Demons *want* you to react to them, to get all bent out of shape and offended. This is the hold they have on the lives of many Christians. Trying to offset their presence in your own strength will never work. God's solution to demonic oppression is that we be strong in the Lord and in the power of His might, not ours. God is *always in control.*

Even if you experience a demonic presence or activity, God is present as well. You are safe, for if you are a Christian, God's Spirit is within you. He is also on the throne of grace and in control of His creation. We are to respond to His presence and learn to place our faith in His reality so we can see with our hearts. The apostle Paul wrote in Ephesians 1:18–23:

> I pray also that the eyes of your heart may be enlightened in order that you may know the hope to which he has called you, the riches of the glory of his inheritance in the saints, and his incomparably great power for us who believe. That power is like the working of his mighty strength, which he exerted in Christ when he raised him from the dead and seated him at his right hand in the heavenly realms, far above all rule and authority, power and dominion, and every title that can be given, not only in the present age but also in the one to come. And God placed all things under his feet and appointed him to be head over everything for the church, which is his body, the fullness of him who fills everything in every way.

God wants us to *respond* to Him—to know He is in control and to maintain our peace. We need to let Him control our fears, our minds, and our hearts. Do this, and the demonic will be disarmed in your life. The oppression may still be there, you may still actually feel their presence, you may even see the results of their activity, but they will not have power over you. The same is true if you are ministering to someone who is oppressed by demons. God is bigger, and the demons have to flee.

The Path to Freedom

I wrote only a portion of what I experienced to highlight key times in my life. My hope was to give you a glimpse of the bondage I once lived in so you would see how Christ has worked in my life and how He used the body of Christ to help me break free of the hold Satan had on me.

Even though I did visit several churches that I couldn't relate to or that didn't meet me where I was, I thank God daily for sending me to Faith Fellowship in Muncie, Indiana, in the autumn of 1981. I thank Him for Harry and Jo Richardson, whom I met there. Their humility and availability allowed God to use them.

After I had been whole for a while, the Richardsons confessed to me that when we first met, they had never encountered anyone quite like me. Jo said they didn't know what to do except to trust God and call on Him for help. And help is exactly what God gave them because, as Jo told me numerous times, He is faithful.

Though they didn't know it at the time, Jo and Harry became instrumental in bringing me to Christ and helping me to grow as a new believer. Although everyone's experience is unique, I have found four clear steps anyone who wants to be free in Christ must take. If God has placed an occultist in your path, it is imperative that they understand the following truths.

God seeks out the lost.

Philippians 1:6 says, "And I am certain that God, who began the good work within you, will continue his work until it is finally finished on the day when Christ Jesus returns" (NLT). God had been working in my life long before I met Him. He pursued a relationship with me before I knew I needed one. He used people around me to remind me of Him and to give me an opportunity to repent of my sin. He *wanted* me to become His child. I have been so encouraged by the realization that in His great love He kept reaching out to me even though I cursed Him. I didn't have to work or strive to earn anything from God.

The occult is very legalistic. An occultist has to have just the right "formula," so to speak, to get an entity to do what he or she wants. It's a legal transaction. But a relationship with God is based on grace. Amazingly I had become God's inheritance: "Moreover, because of what Christ has done, we have become gifts to God that he delights in, for as part of God's sovereign plan we were chosen from the beginning to be his, and all things happen just as he decided long ago" (Eph. 1:11, TLB).

If an occultist truly wants freedom, he must come to understand that God sought him first. He must also understand that he is no longer in control. God, who is good, is in complete control. He wants to teach us to give up the need to control circumstance, people, life—anything. In other words, He wants us to release the need to be our own god.

We are sinners, and we must repent of our sin.

We read in Acts 2:38, "Each of you must repent of your sins and turn to God, and be baptized in the name of Jesus Christ for the forgiveness of your sins. Then you will receive the gift of the Holy Spirit" (NLT). To truly repent and turn to God is to walk away from sin. An occultist will also have to renounce his or her former allegiance to Satan and his kingdom. If I had known I could have had the Holy Spirit living inside me instead of demons, I would have been a Christian long ago. But I lived my life as a temple for demons.

To their credit, the Richardsons did not go looking for a demon-possessed person; when they prayed for me, the demons showed up. Jo told them to go, and they had no choice but to obey. When the demons were gone, I later experienced the baptism in the Holy Spirit. Second Corinthians 6:16 says we are the temple of the living God. The fact that God's Holy Spirit so readily came to live inside me still fills me with wonder. It was so simple. God initiated the relationship. He cleaned me out and filled me with His Spirit. Jo and Harry made sure I knew how to repent and turn to God. Then He gave me a new life just as He promised.

We must submit to the work of the Holy Spirit.

The Bible says, "You are truly my disciples if you remain faithful to my teachings. And you will know the truth and the truth will set you free" (John 8:31–32, NLT). If we are truly to be guided by the Holy Spirit, nothing and no one else can be lord of our lives—neither Satan nor our own selfish desires. Because God wants to guide us through the work of the Holy Spirit, He will tear down anything other than Himself that may be seeking to control us. This is why He confronted the enormous amount of anger I nursed. Yes, I had been wronged, and I felt I had a right to react in anger anytime life did not go my way. But Jo was right when she used to say, "God loves you, but He loves you enough not to leave you the way you are."

By His grace I had experienced a tremendous flood of love from God's presence in my life. If I loved Him in return, I would have to surrender to Him. I had to learn to take my issues to the cross. I *had* to deal with my sin. This is the only way to be set free. Far too many people in this fast-food society want to order up a serving of holiness without putting forth any effort. If you're going to walk, you have to use your legs. If I were to live free of anger, when I felt it bubble up inside of me, I had to choose what the Bible says: "Don't sin by letting anger control you. Don't let the sun go down while you are still angry, for anger gives a foothold to the devil" (Eph. 4:26–27, NLT).

The Holy Spirit wanted me to grow up to be conformed to the image of Christ, and believe me, the Richardsons held me accountable. In the beginning Jo would listen to me as I complained to her, but in her wisdom she would not allow me to remain a child. I'll never forget the day she told me to rely on God, not her; to pull myself up by the bootstraps and be a man. She was tough, but she gave me what I needed. Jo and Harry never stopped telling me that my answer would be found in God and His Word. I believe we would see a lot more people set free if we taught them to rely on an intimate relationship with God and His Scriptures.

We must walk daily with God.

I love 1 Corinthians 1:9: "God, who has called you into fellowship with his Son Jesus Christ our Lord, is faithful." As a child I didn't walk alone. I always knew I had parents who loved me and would support me. But when I accepted Christ, I doubted that He would have my back. After all, I had spent four years actively opposing Him. Why would Jesus listen to me? I thought He would be more inclined to listen to Jo pray *for* me.

Jo would have none of that. Each time I went to her and Harry with a need, they would direct *me* to pray. They would agree with me in prayer, feed me dinner, and then send me home. Jo and Harry wanted me to understand that just about all they *could* do for me was agree in prayer and feed me ham loaf. God is the one I needed to approach for everything else. This has to be the most important thing they did for me. They taught me to rely on God and not on man.

Of course, I would struggle with this at times. How easy it would be if Jo and Harry could just snap their fingers and make the moment's crisis end. But instead they kept pointing me to God and pointing me to God. They would remind me of what kind of Father He is. To this day when life gets tough, in my mind I can see Jo smile. I can hear her favorite expression; "God is faithful."

The wisdom in these two elderly saints lay in the fact that they knew I needed my own personal relationship with God. They knew the only way I would truly be set free was if I experienced Him every day in prayer and in His Word.

Being set free is a lifelong process that is completely attainable. The life of a Christian needs to consist of taking hold of your heavenly Father's hand, learning to trust Him as a child would trust his father, and allowing Him lead you into the freedom only He can provide.

Jeff Harshbarger is the founding president of Refuge Ministries, an outreach he began after leaving Satanism to help others seeking to escape the occult. He holds a master's degree in youth ministry from International Seminary and an additional master's degree in Christian counseling from Bethany Seminary. Jeff has been a guest on TBN, Daystar Television Network, the Miracle Channel, The 700 Club, *and various other television and radio shows. His testimony has been featured in* Charisma *magazine,* The Kingdom of the Occult *by Walter Martin, and* The Unexpected Journey *by Thom Rainer. Jeff is the author of* From Darkness to Light *and is ordained through Calvary Chapel. Refuge Ministries (www .refugeministries.cc) is a member of Evangelical Ministries to New Religions.*

Chapter 2

A SATANIST WHO GREW UP IN CHURCH

By Amber Rane

O NCE YOU HAVE encountered darkness, you never forget it. Once you've stepped into the chasm of violence that lies within the occult, your world is never quite the same. As a former Satanist my world is forever changed. People aren't the same; places have a presence I wish I didn't understand. Yet I am thankful for the awareness I have of the other side. God allows everything to occur for a very specific reason. I pushed and fought against God's love, and He allowed me to delve into a dark realm so that I could see—and so that I could show the world what I saw.

I became a Satanist in the summer of 2004 at the age of fourteen. My background is not wild and horrifying. My parents were both Christians. I grew up in the church. Some of my earliest memories involve lying on the floor under the pews listening to the sermon as I fought the temptation to untie unsuspecting churchgoers' shoelaces. I experienced no real trauma during my childhood other than the deaths of beloved pets. So how did I, a little girl who grew up in church, turn against God in the most direct way possible?

As a child I struggled with anger and violence. I had a mean temper and was told again and again that I needed to calm down and stop trying to push others around—and this was true. However, over time I began to hear another message mixed in with those words, one that said, "You're not strong enough." These were not the words of my parents or those around me. No, these were the words of the enemy.

Being homeschooled and in a family of faithful churchgoers, I learned only the basics of other religions. But I was a thinker. I was always analyzing things and constantly wanting to learn new things. This might seem like a positive trait, but my curiosity often got the better of me. My church and my family were good, but I wanted more—something far more than I had.

As a teenager I was not one of the popular kids, and I knew I probably never would be. It wasn't that I was unpopular; I just went unnoticed. And that was worse than being uncool. I longed to be noticed, to be powerful and special. I wanted to become indestructible. So I began to seek out power that was not of this world.

I turned to things that as a Christian I knew I should avoid. But I thought, "Who would know?" I wasn't being watched like a hawk. So if I stole away into my room to read, who would know that I was studying spirits, ghosts, and demons?

The books I read about the occult told me that people actually talked to these invisible beings, that they were everywhere just waiting for communication. There could even be one next to me right now. *Could I hear them too?* I had to find out, so I kept studying. The more I read, the more I wanted to know. I couldn't get enough.

Before long the voices I wanted to hear were not only audible, but also they were blaring at me. At first I thought it was my own voice in my head telling me I should just die and that everyone else in my life deserved to die with me. But then one night, to my surprise, I heard a voice that sounded distinctly different from my own. Then I heard another voice and another one louder than all the rest. I had found secret friends.

What could be better for a girl who was all alone? Now it wouldn't matter that I had no friends. These voices were better because they were not of this world. My friends were far more powerful than any human around me. I could feel the spirits' fierce anger, and it made me feel strong.

Around this time my family experienced a crisis. But instead of confronting the problem head-on, my parents just began to fight constantly. Now and then one of us kids would try to stop the screaming and door slamming, but usually we would just get pulled into the argument and end up screaming ourselves.

All the while we maintained an image to the outside world that we were a perfect Christian family. That is what made everything so horrible. There seemed to be no way out of the insanity. No one would believe us kids if we were to tell someone how bad things were at home. We felt trapped. So we retreated to our own worlds. It was as though the fear of setting off another argument caused us all to keep a safe distance from one another. None of us kids wanted one parent to think we were choosing the other's side, so we just stayed to ourselves and kept our anger bottled up inside.

Because I longed for stability, I retreated further into the shadows of my bedroom and my relationship with my invisible friends. Satan conveniently waited on my doorstep the entire time, hoping I would give him a chance. Finally I did.

A CHOICE TO REBEL

I knew talking to Satan was wrong. I had been raised in church—I knew better. But I was so angry at what was going on around me that I chose to rebel. The hand that grasped mine to pull me out of my helplessness seemed so comforting and trustworthy, and it made me feel strong instead of weak and worthless. With all the fighting at home, I began to wonder how rebelling against the God my parents served could be a bad thing.

I found strength in paying attention to the voices in my head, and it felt so good to feel strong. My strength made me feel safe. I fed off the voices' anger, and I began to think I had a right to be angry. No one wanted to know me? Fine. I had secret, powerful friends now.

I knew all along that what I was getting myself into was wrong, but I ignored what I learned as a child. Instead of resisting the evil and angry thoughts that raced through my mind, I enjoyed them. Then one day I had my first physical encounter with a demon.

I was heading into my bedroom one night, when the feeling of something cold and dark suddenly stopped me. I was frozen in fear because I knew something dangerous was under my bed. My feelings were so conflicted I thought I must be crazy. How could I be so afraid when this was the very thing I had been wanting?

I went to talk with my mother, but she sent me back to my bed. Feeling like a foolish child afraid of the dark, I jumped into bed and hid under the covers. I couldn't sleep. The thing was too close. But as the hands on my clock moved slowly through the night into the early hours of the morning, an odd thing happened. The fear melted away.

I found myself laughing. I laughed at the absurdity of my behavior. I laughed at my fear. And I laughed because I knew that what I felt was real.

I started to enjoy the darkness and the cold presence that lived there. I reasoned that since what was good hadn't worked, I should seek the opposite. If the presence under my bed was too much to handle, then I would befriend it. I would embrace it.

The voices I had been hearing began to speak clearly to me. They said if I allowed them to give me their power, then people would fear me as I feared them. Desperate for strength I accepted their offer. The next morning I woke up a different person.

Was I possessed? I think so, but not in the Hollywood sense of the word. I was no Emily Rose. Although my inner life completely changed, very few people noticed that anything was wrong with me spiritually. Just as it's not hard to spot someone under the influence of alcohol, it's not hard to spot someone who is under the influence of Satan. But some people can hold their liquor, so to speak, and I was one of them. I could put on a good face. I held it together in church, at youth group, and at home, all the while feeling superior because no one had a clue what was going on inside me.

In reality I had become a person with two personas that

functioned in opposition. I felt as though a new and powerful being had replaced the Amber everyone knew, that the old me had died that fateful night. I began to dress differently, wearing all-black, heavy eyeliner, and boys' clothes. Some people wondered if I had embraced lesbianism, but that was not the case. The new and powerful person or persona I embraced had the strengths of both male and female. I now saw myself as neither gender, and my clothes reflected that.

Yet that new, powerful Amber still felt like the smallest, weakest creature who ever walked the earth. I was strong in public, but when I was alone, the weaker me would surface. I would feel like I was a pathetic loser, a worthless human being who did not deserve to live. Thoughts of suicide played in my mind.

Emotionally I was being played like a puppet. I would go back and forth between the two personas as the demonic spirits made me feel strong then desperately weak. I hated the weak parts of me, so I wanted to get rid of them in any way I could. I craved power, and I craved control. I felt those two traits would make me a destructive force beyond what anyone could imagine. I wanted to destroy, to punish, and to eliminate anyone who got in my way. That is what the darkness promised me—the ability to destroy— and that is what I wanted. Yet while one part of me was greedy for power, the weaker side of me just screamed out for help but was constantly being silenced by the voices of my "friends."

Eventually I could no longer distinguish the demonic voices from my own thoughts, and I began to fear the voices. I would go through my day only half realizing what I was doing, as though I was far away from my actions. I can remember having arguments or hitting my siblings in fits of rage. I would scream at them so loud and long that my throat hurt for days afterward.

Then I began to black out. I would black out of my conscious self just long enough to complete the action. I would hit someone or shout in a rage then return to consciousness and realize in terror what I had done. Everything angered me. My tolerance was at zero.

The smallest, most insignificant things would throw me into uncontrolled fury. I tried to avoid the voices, but I could not. I had completely surrendered to the demon. It took me whenever it chose.

I wasn't violent toward my siblings alone; the demon persuaded me to act violently toward myself. Before I was really aware of what had changed, I had stopped eating. I would go for days without food. I enjoyed denying myself the things we humans need to sustain ourselves. I would rebel against my body whenever I could because I hated God for making me mortal. I wanted to be immortal—and my "friends" promised me that I would be.

Sometimes I would black out from hunger only to come to and find myself eating any food in sight. My hands would shake, and my head would spin in splitting pain. In those moments when my friends let me out of the cage long enough to stay alive, I became more afraid of myself than ever before. I crammed food in my mouth while I shook and shivered.

All I could hear were the conflicting voices saying on the one hand, "You pig. You don't deserve that," and on the other, "You don't need food. You're stronger than that." Far in the back of my mind I would hear the voice of reason, but its words became harder and harder to make out.

I knew that I was dying, but I wanted to die—desperately. By this time my suicidal thoughts were more graphic, more detailed. So many times I would hold in one hand a bunch of pills—blood pressure medication, Valium, and Vicodin (from my parents)—and in the other a cup of water. But I couldn't take my life yet. Satan wasn't through with me. He wanted me right where I was, destroying myself and influencing others.

As each day went by, I became more and more furious at God. I hated Him. I wanted to punish Him—and I know Satan loved it. He wouldn't dare allow me to end my life, not while I was playing so perfectly into his hands. For the time being he was pleased with me.

INITIATION INTO CUTTING

Though I feared my invisible friends, I still loved the darkness. I can't count the number of nights I spent awake, hiding in different dark places around the house at three in the morning. I would look into the darkness and ask it questions. On one night in particular I sat in the living room on the couch staring into the blackness. I sensed a demonic presence off in the corner near the front door. With only the light from outside the living room window between us, I asked it a question out loud.

"What's your name?" The whispered words hung in the air for only a second. A huge and overwhelming wave of fear, unlike anything I had ever experienced before this, swept over me, thick and suffocating. I shivered beneath the blanket I had next to me until I fell asleep. At the time I wasn't sure exactly what the creature's intent was, but now as I look back I know I had made it angry. It growled to silence me and make me feel small. It worked.

By this time my "friends" had already introduced me to the concept of self-injury, not just through starvation but also through cutting. Cutting is a very ugly thing. The moment I drew the blade across my skin, I felt a high that was impossible to ignore. It seemed to heal everything; it made life seem bearable again. But the high wears off after a few seconds, and the despondency that follows makes everything seem worse than before.

The first time I cut myself I used a large needle. Alone in my bedroom, I thought back over my life; I was such a weakling, such a failure. I hated my life. Maybe I should be punished. No, I *knew* I should be punished. So I grabbed the needle and scraped it across my arm.

This would be a kind of initiation. This would prove that I was strong enough to handle pain. And so I began to cut myself on a regular basis. With every red line I cut into my body, I never once thought of the punishment Christ had endured for me. I wasn't interested in hearing that I was forgiven and loved despite my flaws.

I could only long for that moment of ecstasy, which was always followed by crushing depression.

I wanted more than anything to die. I wanted to end this life spent in torment, though I knew I would go on to an eternity of the same. I had burned every bridge. I ran only in the direction my friend, Satan, took me.

For nearly a year I lived in a push and pull of cutting and then trying to stop, only to cut again. Then one day I woke up and realized that my "friend" and its fellow demons were trying to kill me. The cutting had evolved into several near-suicide attempts. And each time I cut, I seemed to be getting closer and closer to a major artery or vein.

I knew I had made the demons angrier. At this point several things in my life had changed. First, I had started dating someone, and because of him I decided to work on my relationship with God. The other influence came from my parents. Despite their problems, they still adamantly insisted that if we obeyed what the Bible said, God would bless and protect us. So I decided to give that a try.

The demons were furious, and they began to attack me in my dreams, showing up in physical form to threaten and hurt me. They told me they wanted me dead and that I could not escape. I spent the next few years in constant fear. They would appear and disappear for varying lengths of time.

I did not have a dramatic experience with light filling my room, but one day I decided to never cut again. Somehow I just knew that the demons wanted to harm me and not help me, and I no longer wanted to cooperate. Of course, this made them retaliate even more, but it soon became clear that they did not have the same hold on me. I would have dreams in which the demons were desperately trying to attack, and I knew this meant they did not have the upper hand they once enjoyed.

Unlike most, I did not experience a moment in which I was suddenly freed from the grip of darkness. I simply began making different choices. One day I decided to never cut again, and later I began to calm my anger instead of allowing myself to fly off in a fit of rage. It took over two years to fully recover from what I had drowned myself in, but here I am today a new person.

To this day it startles me to think how intimate my relationship with darkness was. Like a person recognizing an old friend after many years, I can still see demonic activity when others typically cannot. Yet that is not something I relish. I have lost a great deal. There is so much I wish I could take back, but I cannot.

God has done so much in my life. He has brought me out of darkness and into a new world where there is *light*. His light shines in the darkness, and I'm standing right under the spotlight along with my brothers and sisters in Christ. The journey is not over, and there will be many more obstacles to come, but God is faithful and will see me, and others like me, through.

I became a Satanist at the age of fourteen while part of a Christian family. My time spent in Satanism caused a lot of damage and a lot of pain, but I've come to realize that Jesus was there with me through it all. He never abandoned me. A good father loves and protects his children. Although He may allow His children to stray, He does this so we can know what love truly is.

A LOOK INTO THE DARKNESS

My story is not unique. You probably see hundreds of people every day who are in the same place I once was. They keep their longing for power secret from the world, so you may never suspect that they fellowship with demonic spirits.

Everyone who has ever stepped into darkness has their own story of how Satan pulled them in—some barely saw it coming while others walked into occultism with their eyes wide open. Those who have a background in the church usually have experienced something that turned them away from the faith.

At the age of fourteen I'd had more than my fill of the church, and I rebelled against it and God in my heart. Meanwhile I put on a good face for the congregation and my parents, who would have been ashamed to know I no longer believed. Though I played the part of the obedient church girl, anyone looking for evidence of my double life could have found it.

During my years in the occult I hoped someone would find me and rescue me. I felt weak and thought my only choice was to make friends in high places. The demons promised me strength, and I promised them obedience. They said they'd make everyone pay for everything they did to hurt me, and I swore myself to them.

When I think back on those times when I was in my room at three in the morning, whispering into the darkness to the voices I could hear but didn't always understand, I sometimes wonder how that could have been me. But I've come to realize that anyone is capable of falling into the devil's trap, because our sin nature sets us up to desire the power Satan claims to offer.

Because people usually do not acknowledge the dark possibilities within themselves, they often surprise themselves when they decide to delve into the dark corners of their mind. But we were all born in sin and are capable of even the most heinous acts. The difference is that those in the occult explore those hidden possibilities in their desperate quest for power.

This is a real battle against unseen forces. Satan is claiming souls all around us, even within the church. To resist this satanic assault, we must understand the occult. We must learn to *see*.

Giving Satan leeway in your life isn't as hard as we would like to believe. People act in rebellion toward God on a daily basis. That rebellion comes in many different forms—from telling lies to engaging in sexual sin. Often the individual does not fully realize the torment he has signed himself up for. There is fine print in every agreement, and when someone signs on the dotted line to give Satan control in his life, he ultimately will lose.

Satan wants more than anything to hurt the Father, and what better way than to harm His children? The devil wants to send as many of God's children as possible into eternal fire and punishment.

With every step a person takes away from God, he is aiding Satan in his plot to lash out violently against God.

Satan is a master deceiver. He wants us to believe the Father is really the one to blame for all the evil in the world. After all, if God has so much control, then why are bad things happening? Satan wants us to think that God is a liar, an impotent and apathetic entity who sits up in heaven playing with us like toys for His amusement. Satan is very good at coercing people into believing this by making the mess and blaming it on God.

Satan *knows* he is going to spend all of eternity in violent punishment. As my father always used to tell me, "Satan isn't stupid." In fact, he is very crafty. As a child I never understood this, but now I do. Why would Satan willingly step right into eternal damnation without putting up a fight? He is constantly working to get mankind to rebel against his Creator so he can take as many people as he can down into the flames with him.

WRITTEN IN BLOOD

When I began my dangerous journey into the occult, I signed my name in blood beneath Satan's promise to offer me more strength and power. Those were the terms of our "contract." When I first started cutting, I was just experimenting out of desperation, but it quickly turned into something far more dangerous. Psychiatrists and psychologists have their explanations for why people cut themselves, but there is so much more to this form of self-injury than many of the experts want to see.

The significance of blood goes deep. It represents life, and the Bible declares that without the shedding of blood, there can be no forgiveness of sin (Heb. 9:22). Before Jesus died on the cross to pay the penalty for our sins, God required that the Israelites sacrifice animals to atone for their sins, because blood is the only thing that could purge sin. Blood represents life; sin brings death. We need life to wash away death.

Humanity knows this, and we constantly seek atonement for our faults and shortcomings, and we do this in the strangest ways. Some people understand right away that atonement is found in the literal shedding of blood, but they get confused about *whose blood* must be shed. I was once one of them. I believed the lie that the only way to atone for everything that was wrong with me was to bleed. I couldn't have explained my thinking at the time, but I felt I deserved to be cut into a thousand pieces. I felt I deserved pain. I felt I deserved to bleed.

My thought process was distorted by the lies the enemy was feeding me. What once was black and white became a deep and fuzzy gray that colored my whole world. Did I know cutting was wrong? I guess I did, but I didn't really think much about it. I just felt I had to do it. I needed to pay for everything—everything I did and everything I did not do.

I always felt guilty, which made me want to die and burn in hell. But I also felt an overwhelming fear of being weak, which drove me into survival mode and made me willing to endure almost anything. As you can imagine, these conflicting emotions were ripping me apart from the inside out. Every cut I made on my arms, torso, and legs was a manifestation of that conflict. How could I possibly want to survive? I didn't deserve the air I breathed. How could I possibly want to die? That meant I was giving up—I was weak.

Satan loves to bring confusion and trap people in their most fragile state. If he can make them doubt everything they know to be true, even questioning what is real and what is not, he has them right where he wants them. Satan will use events and circumstances to hurt and confuse his target and then cause them to doubt the truth of God's love and forgiveness. He does this by whispering lies in their ears. After all, he is the master liar (John 8:44).

A very weak follower of Satan named Adolf Hitler once said, "Make the lie big, make it simple, keep saying it, and eventually they will believe it."[1] Where do you think Hitler got this line of thinking? That's easy—from the very angel that rebelled against the

Creator at the beginning of time. Hitler couldn't have deceived millions of people without Satan, and Satan couldn't have destroyed millions of lives without Hitler. The devil needs us to do his dirty work more than he would ever want to admit.

Satan will make a person feel special, desired, and needed just to get his attention. We all want to feel special and wanted. The reality is that we are special; we are necessary. Satan's goal is to make the target believe he is special only to him and the darkness in which Satan thrives. In so doing, he turns that person away from Christ, making him believe God is the enemy and that only Satan's promises are true.

I was convinced that a feeling of release would wash over me like a calming rain the moment I picked up a blade and drew it across my sin. The bright red line would sting but not nearly as much as I wished it would. What I didn't know—what none of the demons wanted me to realize—is that just seconds after the high wore off, an overwhelming feeling of guilt and shame would drown out the momentary relief. The supposed atonement didn't atone for much, so I cut again and again and again and again. I doubted I would ever see the end of that torment. I thought nothing could possibly fix me—nothing.

I had signed a contract with the devil, promising him my allegiance in exchange for power. My debt to him only seemed to increase with each cut. I had written my name in blood all over my frail and fragile body. I had written my name in blood, agreeing to give Satan exactly what he wanted: me.

DESPERATE FOR ATONEMENT

Occultists are desperate for atonement. Through the occult they seek, and presumably find, validation and the power to rise above everyone and everything that has caused them hurt or pain. The power occultists gain from fellowshipping with forces of darkness makes them feel superior, and these feelings of superiority create the illusion of atonement. However, the "power" these demonic forces give comes with serious consequences that can destroy the lives of not only the occultist but also those around him.

Fellowshipping with darkness creates a kind of port within a person. It allows the darkness to work through him and gives others a glimpse of what the darkness is like in human form. These people often look powerful and strong, yet they're constantly fighting against the demons inside them. And because of their false appearance of strength, people follow these "spiritual" leaders in one way or another—whether they're just looking up to them or actually seeking after their "gifts."

Because Satan wants to hurt God, he will kill God's children with God's children. He sends his occult followers out like little grenades to destroy lives. Little by little Satan fills the hearts and souls of so many with violent thoughts and intentions. That violence remains bottled up within and kept secret. What happens when thoughts and feelings that would ordinarily terrify you just fester day after day? This is where the self-punishment begins. And when the occultist realizes that the self-punishment is not offering the atonement he so desperately desires, and when he has exhausted all methods of punishment from Satan's very long list, he will turn outward and punish others while he continues to punish himself.

The occultist caught in this trap sees himself as many pieces put together to form something that resembles a whole, and he develops a divided persona. In punishing himself and others, he plays two roles. One is that of victim, the side of the occultist that disagrees with the punishment he is inflicting. The other is the punisher, the side of the person that is constantly looking for a fight either within himself or with those around him. The complex nature of this conflict is due to the occultist's inability (or rather, unwillingness) to decide which side is in the right.

Because of the incessant demonic attacks he faces, the occultist is in a continual state of confusion and therefore cannot determine which of the many voices is telling the truth. Because he ignored

God's voice, the occultist now hears a thousand other voices screaming out all kinds of conflicting messages.

The punisher gains strength from having a victim, even if that victim is himself. He has someone to push around so he doesn't feel so weak. That is the goal of the punisher side of the individual—to conquer, control, and make everyone pay for mistakes that were made and the pain that was inflicted. The enemy makes the occultist think this strange system creates order in his world, but it actually does just the opposite. It is creating complete disorder. Yet, because the enemy does a good job of hiding the truth, the punisher within the occultist will continue its constant and vengeful mission to defeat everyone and everything that makes it feel threatened. Ultimately, the "punisher" is seeking one thing: power.

POWER

Power is the force driving the occultist. He needs power to survive and get back what he has lost. No one likes to feel weak and helpless, but to the occultist power is a must.

Mankind's desperate pursuit of power began in the Garden of Eden. God created two human beings to love Him. These two creatures were told not to eat of the tree of life, yet they managed to give in to the lies Satan told them—that eating the fruit of the tree would give them power and put them on equal footing with God.

Not only did Satan offer them power, but he also fed them the lie that God was withholding the truth about the tree because He wanted the power only for Himself. In one moment lust poured into Adam and Eve's heart, they tasted sin, and their innocence was lost.

The three players in this tragedy—Adam, Eve, and Satan—all had one goal. They wanted control. Adam and Eve wanted to control their fate and be equal with God. Satan wanted to control the fate of God's children and hurt the Father by leading His children into eternal damnation.

The desire for control can be seen everywhere, every day. It can be seen in severe forms, among the anorexic or suicidal, who resort to desperate measures to control the pain they feel, and in less severe ways, such as in those who tend to dominate a conversation or constantly take charge. We have all felt powerless at some point in our lives, and we will likely feel that way again. There is so much in this world that we cannot control. Those who enter the world of the occult are typically trying desperately to get out of circumstances that created overwhelming feelings of helplessness. But trying to control the uncontrollable can lead to the most devastating consequences.

The truth is, God has given us power. He has given us power to conquer Satan's kingdom in His name and for His glory. Why do so few walk in the power that God has promised? Because the truth about the power we have through Christ is drowned out by the endless din of lies and images of weakness the devil constantly streams into our minds.

As I mentioned before, I was a very angry child, and as I got older, I began to wrestle with violent behavior. I was told again and again that I needed to calm down and stop trying to push others around. This was true. But after a while I began to hear the message that I wasn't strong enough. This was a lie straight from the enemy, but I didn't recognize that at the time. So I grew up feeling as though there was absolutely nothing I could do well.

I believed that the special moments in my life, when I was applauded for something I had done, were meaningless, and the accolades were just lies. I saw myself as having been placed on earth for others' benefit. I lost hope that my life mattered, that I had any value at all—and this lie nearly cost me my life and family.

Ready, Set, Go . . .

I was seconds away from ending my life on multiple occasions, but I was fortunate. My story has a rare happy ending. Too many believers are being lost to Satan because they have so much pain that they don't know how to deal with. We all just want to feel strong and significant. God offers to us all of that and more, but some people cannot see this for themselves. They need to be persistently shown how much they are valued.

The human need to feel strong, to feel important and valued, to feel indestructible is something God has woven into the fabric of our whole being. God wants us, His children, to be strong in the Lord and in the power of His might (Eph. 6:10).

In our human imperfection we often mistakenly search for that strength in the world. I spent six years of my life drowning in an empty existence without God. I spent that time lashing out at Him with every bit of energy I had left in me. Though the temptation exists every day, and the constant messages are blaring in my ears to "come back," I don't want to imagine what it would be like to return to that emptiness.

As believers we are called to be strong for those who can't be, to bear one another's burdens. We must intervene. These children of God who have become slaves to Satan wish more than anything that someone would come alongside them and be strong for them. They know there is more to life than constant threats, fear, and darkness. My life was a sick, violent dance with Satan. I was controlled and used, and I have hurt so many as Satan worked through me.

In 1 Timothy 1:13–14 Paul says to Timothy, "Even though I was once a blasphemer and a persecutor and a violent man, I was shown mercy because I acted in ignorance and unbelief. The grace of our Lord was poured out on me abundantly, along with the faith and love that are in Christ Jesus." He goes on to say in verses 15–16: "Christ Jesus came into the world to save sinners—of whom I am the worst. But for that very reason I was shown mercy so that in me, the worst of sinners, Christ Jesus might display his unlimited patience as an example for those who would believe on him and receive eternal life."

Paul practiced the work of Satan for decades, literally slaughtering

Christians. And here God has transformed him into a disciple, a leader, one who would mentor young Timothy to do even greater works for the Lord. How much greater would this world be if every occultist was shown as much patience and loving pursuit as the Father showed Paul? How many more Pauls would we have running around wreaking havoc on Satan's master plan? We've had some soldiers taken hostage, church. Let's bring them home.

Amber Rane is a psychology major at Lubbock Christian University. She has worked for many years in youth ministry, using the performing arts and writing to express her love and conviction to teens and young adults. Drawing from her experience in the occult, Amber proclaims the truth of God's Word to steer young people away from the darkness and toward Jesus. An author, actor, and director, Amber plans to use her gifts to minister full-time, challenging youth not to compromise the truth.

Chapter 3

SON OF SAM, SON OF HOPE

By David Berkowitz

M Y NAME IS David Berkowitz, and I have been incarcer-
ated since 1977. I was the notorious murderer known as
Son of Sam, and I have been sentenced to prison for the
rest of my life. Yet it was in 1987, when I was living in a cold and
lonely prison cell, that God got hold of my life.

My life had been out of control from the time I was a small
child. I had unexplainable tantrums that made my father pin me
to the floor until I calmed down. In school I was so violent that
once a teacher had to put me in a headlock and throw me out of
the classroom. Even at a young age I was plagued with bouts of
severe depression. My parents took me to a child psychologist once
a week for two years, but the therapy sessions had no effect on my
behavior. I would sit on the window ledge of our sixth-floor apartment with my legs dangling over the edge and think about suicide.
My parents had me talk to a rabbi, teachers, and school counselors.
Nothing worked.

When I was just fourteen, my mother died. For the most part she
had been the source of whatever stability I had. I was filled with
anger at her death and became even more depressed, even though
my dad helped as best he could. Immediately out of high school I
went into the Army and somehow managed to finish my three-year
enlistment.

In 1974 I was out of the military and living alone in New York
City. The next year I met some guys at a party who were heavily

involved in the occult. Having always been fascinated with witch-craft and other forms of the occult, I felt drawn into Satanism. I began reading the Satanic bible and innocently practicing various rituals and incantations. I did not know I was headed down the road to destruction.

Eventually I crossed the invisible point of no return and committed horrible crimes that resulted in my taking the lives of six people. In 1978 I was sentenced to 365 years in prison. I was then declared insane and sent to a psychiatric hospital before being sent back to prison.

Ten years passed, years lived in deep despondency and without hope. Then one cold winter evening I was walking the prison yard when another inmate introduced himself and began telling me how Jesus Christ loved me and wanted to forgive me. I mocked him, thinking that God could never want anything to do with me. But this man did not give up.

We became friends and walked the yard together while he shared what Jesus had done in his own life. He said Jesus Christ had died on a cross for all the sins that I had committed and would forgive me if I put my faith and trust in Him. He gave me a Gideon pocket-size New Testament and asked me to read the Psalms. I read from them every night, and God began to melt my stone-cold heart.

One night while reading Psalm 34, I came upon the sixth verse, which says, "This poor man cried, and the Lord heard him, and saved him out of all his troubles." Everything hit me at once—the disgust at what I had become and the guilt over what I had done. Late that night I got down on my knees in my cell and cried out to Jesus Christ. I told Him that I was sick and tired of doing evil. I asked Jesus to forgive me for all my sins.

After praying for quite some time, the heavy but invisible chain that had bound me for so many years was broken. Peace flooded over me. I did not understand what was happening, but I knew in my heart that my life would be different from then on.

Today I have an outreach ministry right here in prison. I work with men who have various emotional and coping problems and pray with them as we read our Bibles together. I have worked as the chaplain's clerk, and I also have a letter-writing ministry. Through television appearances I have been given the opportunity to share with millions how Christ has delivered me and given me a new life.

One of my favorite Bible passages is Romans 10:13. "For whosoever shall call upon the name of the Lord shall be saved" (KJV). This makes it clear that God has no favorites but welcomes all who call upon Him. I was once a Satan worshipper and a murderer, but my life now is proof that Jesus Christ can bring about forgiveness, hope, and change. No longer am I the "Son of Sam" but the "Son of Hope."

I was involved in the occult, and I got burned. I became a cruel killer and threw away my life and destroyed the lives of others. Now I have discovered that Christ is my answer and my hope. He has turned me from a path leading to eternal damnation in the lake of fire to the blessed assurance of eternal life in heaven. He can perform the same kind of transformation in anyone's heart!

In the 1970s David Berkowitz gained notoriety after he ruthlessly took the lives of six strangers. Prior to that time he became fascinated with witchcraft and eventually began practicing Satanism. David was sentenced to life in prison, but ten years into his incarceration a fellow inmate told him about the forgiveness available through Jesus Christ. Alone in his cell David cried out to Jesus. It was the beginning of his new life. Today he has an active prison ministry, leading Bible studies and prayer groups.

Chapter 4

GRACE CHANGES EVERYTHING

By Becky Hutchinson

This testimony is dedicated to my best friend, Katie Dorsey,
who died of cancer March 24, 2011.

I ACCEPTED JESUS CHRIST as my Lord and Savior Easter 2006. But for the grace of God, this radical life change almost didn't happen. I believe we are born sinners, but I don't believe we are born alcoholics, drug addicts, homosexuals, or any other addictive lifestyle we may find ourselves trapped in. I share this as my own personal reminder. The circumstances I was born into, though devastating, did not make me choose Satanism, nor did they keep me there till it almost killed me.

I was a child of severe abuse and was left an orphan. This shaped my mind-set toward people and God. It shaped the way I felt about myself. I was extremely fearful of everything and full of anger. I had no concept of love. I trusted no one, and I blamed myself for the pain and hurt I experienced at the hands of others.

I took this outlook on life into several foster homes, the last of which I entered after having been hospitalized for severe burns and emotional scars too deep to fathom. After this physical and emotional trauma, I was placed into a somewhat Christian home. My mom attended church and was Christian; my dad didn't go to church, but he was a loving and caring man. This home was an amazing change for me. These people actually told me they loved me, and they shared the wild idea that God loved me too.

Every day they said it. Every day. I couldn't comprehend it. So I pushed them away.

They didn't give up on me, though, and several years later they adopted me. I couldn't believe they wanted to keep me. I was used to being shuffled from home to home. Because of their commitment I made progress in allowing them to love me. Forget God, though. I wanted no part of God or church. My mom would take me to church at times, and I would just leave. People never took the time to get to know me. I felt they just judged me as a sinner. Instead of hearing messages about how much Jesus loved me, I often heard the classic line, "If you don't get saved, you are going to hell."

This was the start of my learning to hate church, God, and Christians. I lived through abuse (physical and emotional), and I hated myself, blamed myself—and now these Christians were saying if I didn't accept God, I'd get punished? The choice was not hard for me to make: not interested.

I chose the people and friends who seemed to share my outlook on life. We were the rebellious kids. We abused alcohol and drugs, and we loved rock music. Alcohol became my best friend through my teenage years. It covered up the pain and despair I felt inside. In retrospect, I believe it kept me alive long enough to find a different way.

My parents loved me through all this. At times I couldn't understand why they didn't call social services and send me away like everyone before. My teen years were one big party, and I got into some of the darker elements of pop culture. I loved dark music—Black Sabbath, Iron Maiden—and I loved scary movies. Both reflected my inner feelings. I was an extremely angry, sometimes depressed, often suicidal individual. I had the perfect mind-set for being drawn into the occult.

I'm sharing parts of my early life because it's important people know that some individuals are more easily drawn into cults. The saying that "If you don't stand for something, you will fall for anything" really applied to my life. I didn't stand for anything. I was so swayed by my despair, anger, and hate to be involved in anything like love or God.

After high school I enlisted in the Navy. I completed boot camp and was stationed in Hawaii. Once I got settled in at work and my surroundings, it didn't take long for me to find the clubs and the alcohol. I wouldn't say I was an alcoholic yet, but I sure needed alcohol to feel OK. Around me were people who loved the same lifestyle. I had Christian friends who at times would invite me to church, but I had no desire to go.

My introduction into the occult happened slowly. I started hanging out with certain people at a club I visited. These friends were involved in some kind of group. One night, in a club down in Waikiki, a man named Michael joined me at the bar for a beer. We talked about nothing serious—he was just a really nice guy who shared a beer and complimented me, making feel special.

What I know now is it was all a game, a way to pull me slowly in, gain my trust, show a little care, and pretend to be my friend. Michael provided the things I needed on the inside, and he won me over. My life changed but not for the better. I hung out all the time with my new friends, partying and club-hopping.

When we hung out at Michael's condo, we talked about life and what we believed as far as people, religion, and God goes. Michael was really interested by what I believed. As I look back, it was his way of seeing if I would make it in the occult. I was a great prospect because I had no belief in God or religion, and most of the people in my life hurt me.

This is the time when I truly became addicted to alcohol. About a month after meeting these people I was talked into leaving the base and moving in with Michael and several others. They wanted me, so I packed up and moved.

Michael was much older than all of us, and he wasn't in the military. He was from California and had studied at the Church of

Satan. Michael was a high priest in the occult. Learning this really unlocked my fascination for dark things. I had seen Satan stuff in movies, and as a teen I listened to dark music, but deep down never believed in him or knew that people actually worshipped him. I thought Satan was a lot like Santa Claus or the Easter Bunny. People made him up to scare others and to make good horror movies.

For the next six months I never once was able to attend Michael's occultist meetings with him. He told me when the time was right he would let me come and watch. He said I could ask him questions later about what happened at them.

At home we dabbled in tarot cards and hypnotism, and we read literature on cults and satanic worship. I had an overwhelming desire to know more, and I felt at times a soft voice pulling me deeper into it. I witnessed people become hypnotized to the point where they actually hurt themselves with knives. For some reason I could not be hypnotized. Michael tried and became irate that my mind was closed to it. I wasn't trying to be closed. Hypnotism just never "took" with me.

A Small Black Book

I went to work as usual, but my attitude became negative toward my job, being in the military, and life in general. I had nightmares almost every night. I dreamed of monsters, killings, and death. I'd wake up in the middle of the night sweating and scared. The dreams became more graphic the deeper I got into the occult.

When Michael began asking me to visit different places with him, that's when I finally was able to talk about what I thought of all this. At that time my curiosity outweighed my fear. I wasn't convinced this occult stuff was real. Michael took me to witchcraft stores, where he purchased candles and other items needed for their ceremonies and group meetings. I watched, feeling this occult stuff was more fantasy than reality. Wow, was I wrong.

The longer I stayed in these occultist environments, the more

Satan showed me he was alive and well. One day on one of our road trips Michael handed me a small black book. "Read it. Study it. Let me know what you think," he said. It was *The Satanic Bible* by Anton Szander LaVey.

The Satanic Bible was very hard to understand because I had never read the Bible, and *The Satanic Bible* is a mockery of God's Word. Nonetheless, I became addicted to the book. I read, studied, and asked a lot of questions. Today I don't remember everything verbatim, but I do remember the key points. There were chapters that represented the elements fire, air, earth, and water.

Fire was the "Book of Satan," and air was the "Book of Lucifer." Earth was the "Book of Belial," and water was the "Book of Leviathan." Satanists consider themselves gods. The title "Church of Satan" was a mockery of the Christian church just by calling itself a church. I remember a chapter that took every beatitude and mocked each one. Michael had me study the Book of Leviathan because we read from it at every Black Magic ceremony. Michael also had me study how we set up the room because our ceremonies had an order to them.

This life was new and exciting. I was wanted. I had friends, so I went along with anything they asked. The coven I was in did not push anyone to participate in anything sexual. Michael told me the Church of Satan in California *did* use sexual sacrifices, and he told me a lot of their altars involved women as the altars because women represented the earth. I am so thankful I didn't have to suffer that type of abuse. I'd been sexually abused at the age of twelve, so I was already traumatized. God was gracious to keep me from further sexual abuse.

Everything in the ceremonies was black. The only lights were candles, and they were black. The clothing worn by the priest and others was black. My heart and mind grew to match the darkness. I don't remember a lot (and I know that's a blessing from my Savior), but I retain the memory of a bell being rung, and through writing this chapter I remember that the bell was rung to start a ceremony and to end it.

After six months of reading and studying *The Satanic Bible*, I was taken to my first ceremony to observe. Not long after Michael deemed me ready to become the reader during the ceremony. Our cult took a whole lot from the Church of Satan and *The Satanic Bible*, but Michael added things to our group that at the time seemed exciting but later haunted me. Satanic worship, I discovered, was based on us becoming our own gods. I learned that being your own god meant dismissing the notion that you needed any other god. I decided who was lovable and who was dispensable through curses performed through magic. There were no sins because I had no one to answer to. Weakness was a liability.

The only true way I could become what Michael wanted me to be was to let Lucifer have my life, totally and completely. Once a month we had a ceremony for those who were ready to give themselves wholly to Lucifer and to the cult. The night when it was my turn to surrender, I felt nervous. Even after being with these people for seven months and desiring to belong, I was still scared. I was a self-reliant person, and the occult was asking me to give my will over to something I wasn't sure about and to place myself under the authority of someone who I wasn't sure would lead my life in a good direction.

I traveled with Michael that night to our meeting place. The black candles were lit. The altar of Baphomet was always used in our rituals, and this was no exception. Dressed in black cloaks, Michael and a few others led the ritual. Michael cut his arm and bled into the chalice. He offered words to me, the group, and Satan. In turn I had to offer to the group my total dedication, and to Satan I offered my life. The chalice was passed to each of us, and we had to take a sip of human blood. To end the ceremony Michael offered a hail to Satan, and we as a group followed. I was then a complete Satanist and belonged to a cult. My life changed for the worse, but I didn't recognize it until almost a whole year later.

People at work noticed because my behavior reflected the change in my heart. I felt the evil inside of me and heard voices all the time. I wasn't mentally ill in the medical sense; I was spiritually ill. Sometimes something would take over, and I would surrender to it. I became totally engrossed in the occult and my group. I studied and went to all the ceremonies and rituals. I remained a reader and grew a lot closer to Michael. We never crossed over into a sexual or romantic relationship; we just got really close like a brother and sister.

The wild parties at our condo featured drugs and alcohol. We invited many people—some military, some not; most were just friends. Our parties got borderline crazy, and I saw people get hurt because they would partake of stuff they knew nothing about, thinking it a joke, then finding out later that dabbling in the occult was dangerous for the average person.

One night I invited a friend to one of our parties. When I wasn't paying attention, she ingested some pills and then let Michael hypnotize her. The whole thing went bad, and she became out of control. A friend of mine purposely locked her in a closet just to keep her safe. I had the bright idea to let her out, thinking I would just take her back to the base. What a mistake that was.

As soon as I opened door, she took off running, out the condo door and toward a balcony. We were located eighteen floors up, and in her distorted frame of mind, she thought she could fly. At the last second I ran and kind of jumped at her legs. By God's grace I grabbed her ankles and pulled her to the ground before she went over. I calmed her down enough to get her to my vehicle and drive her back to the base.

Thank God the next day she didn't remember anything that happened that night. I think I was happy about her memory lapse. My group couldn't afford bad publicity. We did not need the police around because of something as trite as drugs and alcohol use. Nothing should interfere with our worship. We continued to hold parties, but Michael and the others refrained from letting non-group members participate.

There was a young woman living at the condo. She came and went a lot while I was there that first year. She'd leave for a few weeks and then return. One evening she told me she wanted out of the occult, but every time she left something pulled her back. She told me she went to California and checked out the main Church of Satan, where she asked a man how to get out. He said, "You can never leave. You can leave physically, but mentally and spiritually you will always belong to Satan and the occult."

I laughed, not believing what he said. Soon, however, I learned that it was the honest truth. Without meeting with Jesus, I would have died and gone to hell.

This young woman disappeared for the longest time. Then one day I saw her sitting on the beach with a Bible held tightly in her arms. I asked where she had gone and what she was doing with the Bible. She hoped this Bible would save her and was carrying it around as protection. I talked her into coming back to the condo instead of living homeless on the beaches. She moved back in. A week later we found her dead in the bathtub. She had cut her wrist and the main artery in her neck. She bled out by herself while we all slept.

The Beginning of the End

This was the beginning of the end. The incident put us on the radar of the police and the military. Before this incident the Navy had received some words of concern about me. People were worried about where I lived, as they could not figure out what I was into.

During the next month, without my knowledge, my fellow Navy members worked to force me out of the condo and back into base housing. I was presented with a document signed by a military judge forcing me back onto the base. I was not a happy person, but I complied. When I look back, I think I was relieved because the life I was living, especially after the suicide, didn't leave me feeling good inside.

Back at the base I didn't have a roommate, which was good because I had loud, very realistic nightmares. I began to use alcohol and pills to remain asleep.

My forced move did not keep me from my cult friends or the occult practices. I continued to hang out and party. I continued to attend rituals and talk with Michael. The Navy tried to send me to counseling, but I refused to go. It didn't take long, however, for my alcohol abuse to get me in some minor trouble, and I was forced to go to counseling anyway.

Weekly counseling for me was a joke, because I didn't want it. I refused to talk. During this time I went to work, did my job, and kept my supervisors off my back. I had a really good friend on base who was a Pentecostal Holy Roller; that's what I called her. Pam tried to share God with me all the time. She'd come by my room and bring friends from her church. I was polite, but Pam and her friends scared me. When they were around, my whole insides would go crazy.

I was invited to church, but I didn't go. I was already anti-God, but now I became really angry, very anti-Christian and anti-church. I found myself saying hurtful things to anyone who mentioned God to me. I went out of my way to tell anyone who would listen how much I hated God, Christians, and church. This cycle grew stronger over the years, and along with the darkness already inside me, I was on a crusade to prove God wasn't the answer.

The alcohol abuse got worse, not just because I liked to party but because I was out of control. I got to the point where I went to Michael and told him I wanted out. I told him from this point on, I wanted nothing to do with Satan and nothing to do with God.

Michael and a few others tried to convince me to come back, but I couldn't take it anymore. I had nightmares, anger, and I didn't sleep well. My whole life was crazy. I really believed if I said I wanted nothing to do with either God or Satan, they both would just leave me alone. I was so wrong. God was after me through Christians, and Satan was after me through my mind, feelings, and dreams. I bounced for the next year and a half in and out of counseling.

People told me I was an alcoholic, and that was my problem. Well, yeah, alcohol was a big problem, but Satan was the main problem. Today I know Jesus was the answer. I used alcohol as a painkiller, sleep aid, and means of cutting off the voices in my head. I thought of suicide a lot; life was just hard to live. I never went back to the cult or any occultist meetings, and I've never seen Michael again. But I didn't stop reading about the occult.

My discharge date arrived, and I couldn't wait to just go home. I honestly believed inside that if I left Hawaii, everything I experienced would stay there. I arrived home in 1985, and for a while my life was calm, and it really seemed like everything would be OK, but I was wrong.

The Bible says that when evil spirits are cast out or removed, and you replace them with nothing, they return, sometimes more powerful. "When an evil spirit leaves a person, it goes into the desert, seeking rest but finding none. Then it says, 'I will return to the person I came from.' So it returns and finds its former home empty, swept, and in order. Then the spirit finds seven other spirits more evil than itself, and they all enter the person and live there. And so that person is worse off than before" (Matt. 12:43–45, NLT). What I needed was for Jesus to replace the hole, but that wasn't going to happen for almost twenty more years.

I found an awesome job and got a new car, and life seemed great. At my job I was the model employee. That is how I lived my life all the time. I always made sure my outside world looked perfect. To others my life seemed awesome, but all they saw was the outside. The outside means nothing if the inside is a mess. For the next ten years I worked at the same job, I drank on and off, and I connected on and off with the world of the occult. Depression and suicidal thoughts became an everyday thing.

The nightmares continued. Sometimes they seemed to cross over into my reality. I kept having vivid dreams of a man in black. He would come every night in my dreams, and he always did violent things to the people I loved. The man in black looked a lot like the satanic worshippers from our rituals and ceremonies. He also looked like an executioner. I was never able to see his face.

This man from my dreams began to cross over into my real life. It was terrifying. I started to hear him in my head, and I would catch glimpses of him, mostly at night. One night in particular I woke up from a nightmare, and he was standing in my bedroom. I started screaming and throwing stuff at him. Needless to say everyone in my home came running to find my room a mess and no one there but me. I knew deep inside that he was there and that he was real and that he was straight from the gates of hell. Those closest to me seemed to think I was going crazy, and I don't disagree. I had mental issues brought on by the life I chose to live. But this was also a spiritual battle going on for my soul and ultimately my life.

I knew only the dark side, Satan, or Lucifer. I had not yet met the Savior, but He was still fighting for me. So I worked, I partied, I drank, and I fell deeper into the abyss. At home, as in the military, I had friends who attended church and professed to be Christians. They told me they prayed for me. I told them thanks but no thanks because I thought prayer was useless on me, that they should save it for someone who really needed it.

I started to see changes in my behavior when I drank. I grew up angry, and that anger was always inside directed at me. I never let my emotions show, and my body couldn't hold it any longer. At clubs I started to become explosive. I had minor run-ins with the police, and I was belligerent with them as well. At times I was a walking time bomb because of the lack of sleep and all the feelings inside me.

I was ready to self-destruct. Most days I thought about suicide. It was a constant battle between the demons inside me and my attempts to cope enough to not blow my head off. In the beginning alcohol had acted as a lifesaver. Yet at this point the alcohol didn't work anymore. It only made me more depressed.

I guess it was during the early nineties that some concerned people intervened. Several times they checked me into the hospital to have my head examined with regard to my thought process and my drinking. My friends meant well. I ended up in the hospital several times over the next few years. Usually I stayed about thirty days. I would be put on medication, and I would throw it away. They recommended counseling, but when I was released, I never went. I couldn't even think of telling the truth. I could never betray Satan or the occult. Even though I was no longer active, I knew if I told anyone what I was about, Satan or his demons would end my life. Fear kept me silent.

I remember coming home one evening and something told me to burn a Bible in my parents' home. I took the family Bible that belonged to my mom to the backyard and set it on fire. I stood there, laughing until I looked around and saw my mom. It was only then that I realized what I was doing. I did not have an answer for her that night. I was shocked too. Then I began to have memory lapses, almost like amnesia. It felt at times like someone else was directing my every move.

In 1994 I decided suicide was the only way out for me. I wrote a note one evening and left it where my family would find it. I got a bottle of pills and some beer to wash them down with. I left in my car and turned the music up loud, but I couldn't drown out the voice screaming in my head, "You must die!"

I don't remember much from that night, just driving, drinking beers, and swallowing pills. When I came to, I was in an emergency room in Virginia, and I was hooked up to a bunch of machines. My journey had taken me from Maryland to Virginia. Someone later told me that I was in a nightclub in Virginia and had collapsed on the dance floor.

When I got out of intensive care and was placed in a regular room, I wanted to go home. I was told, however, that I would be placed in a hospital in Virginia, against my will, to get more help. I tried to escape, but the police made sure I was taken to Dominion Hospital. At the hospital I was placed in an open ward along with a lot of other people. Most were really sick mentally. I spent more than thirty days at Dominion and then was placed in an intensive care unit for religious abuse.

I couldn't take it. The groups and individual counseling constantly upset me. They talked of God, and I felt as though they were trying to convert me. They insisted that in just one month, if I accepted God, my life would be all better. I refused to share and often walked out of the groups. The anger and memories were too much, and the "God talk" only intensified the feelings. I received a diagnosis, and they wanted me to take various medications. I refused and fought them over it all. I told my counselor that my problems were not mental, and medication wasn't going to change a thing.

After my time in the hospital I was told I could not go home because I was a threat to myself. I had two choices: I could be placed in a longer term hospital or I would go to a woman's home in Virginia, where I would be required to take medication. Before I could go home, I would have to complete their program. I thought of ways to run, but I couldn't hide forever. Deep down I knew I needed help. I knew this all along; I was just scared to death.

I moved into the home but was kicked out a month later because of my nightmares and angry outbursts. The people there believed I wasn't in the right place to receive the help I needed. This had been the story of my life since as far back as I could remember.

People meant well, and the help offered to me was awesome. I am thankful today for all the positive seeds that were planted in my heart and soul. But as awesome as the help was, it wasn't the answer for my life. The answer wasn't found in a pill. And even though drugs and alcohol were a problem, the answer wasn't in rehabs. The answer was the one thing I learned to hate, the one thing I thought I could never have.

I had been taught for years that once you give your life to Satan, you belong to him and him alone. I believed you could never walk away. Several years later I found Jesus Christ. Yet a huge stumbling block in my life, and I imagine in the lives of others, is the big lie that you can never leave the occult. It's brainwashing at best with a bit of reality. Satan and hell are as real as God and heaven. I don't know how many people of faith I crossed paths with over the years. They would give me a gospel tract or get into a huge debate with me, which always came down to them telling me that without Jesus I was going to hell. Well, for all my life, hell was living inside of me.

A Temporary Fix

I eventually left Virginia and went home. At least I wasn't drinking, and for a while my life seemed changed. This was just a temporary fix. They sent me home with medication, which I threw away. As far as alcohol and other drugs were concerned, I left them alone more out of fear than anything else. But about a month later I was bored. It didn't take me long to hook up with old friends and start dabbling in occult practices and going out to clubs. I wouldn't drink while at the clubs, but that didn't last long either. I was so addicted to that high. I thought I needed it to keep me calm and to control the fear that the demons would attack me.

In 1996 I met a man named Joe, who was a Christian. He was also a recovering alcoholic. We met through a mutual friend, and I thought he was a decent guy. I never felt threatened by his Christianity. We always had deep discussions about our lives and what we believed. I trusted him enough to share just little of my past with the occult and my fears. Joe shared a little about his sister. She had some similar stories, just not as long or intense.

One time I shared my nightmares and my fear of being killed or taking my life. Joe called me soon after and asked if I was ready to get some real help. Joe had a minister friend who counseled on the side. If I was willing, I could meet him to see if we clicked. Then maybe I could start working on some of the occult issues I had. I asked Joe to let me think about it. I was absolutely not interested in becoming a Christian. I just needed the nightmares and suicidal thoughts to go away.

Joe called me one night in January to see if I was ready to start counseling once a week. He told me that his pastor-friend was willing to meet with me to discuss his services for counseling. We would just talk and work through some of my issues. I said I would be willing to meet the man as long as Joe came with me. Preachers caused me great fear.

The plan was on that coming Friday night, Joe would take me to the pastor's home. The pastor had told Joe that he was having people over from his church for a get-together that evening. If we could come around nine that night, it would be great.

I remember the night like it was yesterday. It was cold and raining, and I was scared to death. I hadn't told anyone where I was going. I drove myself because Joe, who was married, didn't want to be alone in his car with a female other than his wife.

We finally arrived at this huge white home with black trim and black window frames. I walked up to the door with Joe, and a woman answered. She invited us inside to a house full of people. As soon as we entered the room, the people looked at me as if I had the plague, said good-bye, and walked out. I found myself sitting alone at the kitchen table with Joe and the man who introduced himself as Joe's pastor. The pastor asked us to follow him to his den in the back of the house.

Once back there I sat on a love seat, Joe sat across the room, and the pastor sat nearby. Then the pastor moved to the table right in front of me. He asked me if I was possessed by Satan. I laughed, and before I could speak, he lunged forward. He put his hand on my forehead and pushed my neck back onto the couch back, yelling all this stuff.

I have vivid memories of him yelling Bible stuff and looking like some crazy person. I started fighting to get him off of me, but it was useless because of the way he had my head pinned. I yelled for Joe to help me, but he never responded.

The pastor finally let go of my head. I stood up yelling at him. He pushed me back down.

Joe sat with his head bowed and his eyes closed, so I suppose he was praying. He was definitely not helping.

I kept yelling at the pastor. I called him crazy and asked if this was how he helped all the people who came to see him.

I kept trying to get out. But then the doorbell rang, and in walked two huge men carrying Bibles and two bottles of some kind of liquid. They tied me up and made me stand. And over the next hour I was soaked in this oil-like substance from head to toe. Both bottles were emptied on me.

They yelled at me and tried to get me to read from the Bible. At this point I was so angry that I kept fighting and cursing all of them. The more I fought, the worse it got. But I wasn't about to back down. This was so wrong! I knew their God would never do this to a human being. I started kicking at them, so they tied my legs together. At one point I remember the pastor trying to rub a cross into my forehead.

They all circled around me and began singing and reading, and they demanded that I confess Jesus as my Savior. I refused, and they threw me back on the couch. They beat me and jerked me around for more than five hours. Finally, at four in the morning, they set me free. I ran to my car and took off as fast as I could. Once on main road I figured out where I was and headed toward home.

I couldn't drive well because I was soaked in oil, and I believe I was in shock. I drove to a friend's home and rang her doorbell. After she got over the shock of seeing me in my condition, she called the police. They took a report.

I needed medical attention, so my friend took me to the hospital. The hospital cleaned me up. I had a cut on my forehead, and my right wrist was badly sprained. So, once again, my life was totally shaken up. This time it came from someone I trusted and from people who claimed to be Christians.

This incident threw me into a deep depression on top of all the wounds from the occult. My fear of God and the church was intensified by this incident. Instead of getting the help I so badly needed, I was pushed deeper into hate. I decided once again that I wanted nothing to do with God, Satan, Christians, and the church. I would be an atheist and would never ever trust anyone again.

The police report went to the state's attorney. Once charges had been filed for kidnapping, assault, and religious abuse, my home phone went crazy. I received threats, and people called all hours of the day and night. They called me the antichrist and other horrible names. Finally we had to change our number. I went to see a lawyer. He decided that we needed to take the case out of the county because the people would turn it into a witch hunt against me. It was almost a year before any kind of justice was served. Really, the justice didn't come close to the crime committed and the damage it did to my spirit.

The case was settled out of court, and monetary rewards were issued to me along with some other judgments against the people involved. But I was the one who had to live and suffer each day after that. I didn't know how to put the hatred and anger behind me. The feelings festered and grew stronger and stronger, until I could not sleep at all. I was consumed with thoughts of revenge. I sat in my home and planned how to make the pastor suffer as I had.

So one night, running on no sleep, anger, and hatred, I decided that he needed to die. Over the next two weeks I planned how to do it. I convinced two other people to drive me and be lookouts. I chose the night, and off we went. I don't remember a lot about what happened once we got near his home, but I do remember the German shepherd that pinned me near a fence and the police officer who I didn't know lived on the same road.

I was charged with trespassing and released. Thank God my intentions were never discovered. I honestly wanted that pastor to help me. Because of ignorance on his part, because he did not understand what he was dealing with, I continued to be plagued by fear and nightmares.

Life went on, and I managed to keep myself together to the best of my ability. Ironically, in 1999, a friend of mine called me and asked if I liked working with kids. I told him yes and asked why he wanted to know. He said that the director of a day care at the Baptist church needed a helper, and he thought of me. The job sounded great, but the location was not too appealing. I couldn't see myself walking in a church ever again.

But the job was located in a huge room, in the back part of the church, and the hours were great, so I took it. This was definitely God working without my knowledge. He put me in a Baptist church, working with kids. As I look back, I can see part of His plan for my life.

I worked at that job for almost seven years, and over those seven years I slowly heard the Word of God. I had numerous talks with Christians who didn't hurt me. I met a pastor who became my friend, and over time I asked him a lot of questions.

While I was there, I met my best friend. Katie was a Christian, and she accepted me the way I was, flaws and all. She never judged me, and we remained the best of friends until she died in March 2011. Katie became my sounding board. I bombarded her with questions, argued with her, and I am sure at times I upset her. But Katie always showed me love. She never hurt me, and she never left my side.

In 2004 my beautiful Christian mother got very sick. I worked and took care of her when she needed it. By the end of 2004 she ended up in the hospital. Her church sent people to visit with her, and they would pray. When they did, I would leave the room because I didn't want to be around it. Mom seemed to feel worse every time they would come. I decided God was getting back at me first for being a Satanist and now an atheist.

I wanted to tell all of them to never come back, but Mom loved them. She believed in God and prayer. My mother died on February 21, 2005. Before she passed away, she took my hand and told me she was going home to see Jesus. She died with peace in her heart, and I knew she had something I didn't.

FINDING ANSWERS

After her death and burial I took about a week off and then I went back to work. I wasn't dealing at all with my grief, and one day one of the leaders called me into his office. He old me I needed some help, and he sent me to see an awesome woman named Chris. Chris was a counselor with Christian Life Counseling Center. I remember the first time we met. I was afraid, but she had a peace and love for people that I could feel. I believe God let me see and feel it because this was part of His plan for my life.

I saw Chris once a week, and although I was terrified, I somehow knew she had the answers. I just knew she wasn't going to hurt me, that she'd be different.

This was a Christian counseling service, and I asked Chris if I could come since I still wasn't a Christian. Of course, she told me yes. Chris said the counseling service was considered Christian because the counselors were and the program was Bible-based. The most important thing was that I would hear about God and Jesus. I told her I needed help, but I didn't need God and I really didn't want to hear about Him every week. She didn't agree, and I was OK with that.

Being sent or recommended to go to Christian Life Counseling was the beginning of a long journey of healing for me. God placed me in the care of an amazing woman who knew how to reach me gently. Over a span of almost two years we took one day at a time and, sometimes, just hours at a time.

Things didn't always go smoothly in counseling because I fought it a lot. At times I listened to her tell me about Jesus or read from the Bible. Other times I blocked it out and became angry.

Chris used every available resource, including the experience of other Christians who had lived a life similar to mine. We went through my addictions and the occult; she prescribed medications when I needed it, and, most of all, we spent a lot of time in prayer. Chris showed me Jesus. I saw His love and care shinning through another. I was a beat-up, hurting, and very angry human being who was dying slowly—not from a physical illness but from a life and sin issue. Without intervention my life was going to end—and by my own hands.

It took almost a year, a rough year, but I became more and more open to the things of God. Once I truly realized that Chris wasn't going to hurt me and that God didn't want to hurt me, I began to let God in a little at a time.

Breaking through the occult issue was tough. It was probably the toughest battle I have ever been in, but I didn't go through it alone. I realize today that there were a lot of people praying for me and reaching out to me.

The year 2006 came around, and I was still seeing Chris. I wanted to attend church—what a concept! I didn't have a clue where to go or what to do. God reached out again to me.

Through Chris I met Jeff Harshbarger, another awesome Christian, who had much the same background as I did. We began to chat online, and I saw that we had a lot in common. One day out of the blue Jeff asked me if I'd ever heard of Calvary Chapel churches. I told him no. He said he attended a Calvary Chapel church and that he would check to see if there were any where I lived. Once again God was working for me. A Calvary Chapel church was very near my home. Jeff asked if I was ready to try church out.

It was much easier said than done. This was the next toughest thing I had ever done in my life. My friend contacted some people at this local church, and he told me they would call me before Sunday and help me out when I arrived. This was a very long and scary week for me. I hadn't stepped foot in a church since I was really young, and I was terrified.

That Saturday my phone rang, and I saw that the ID said Calvary Chapel. I almost couldn't pick up the receiver. The caller on the other end was the pastor of the church. He spoke to me for a while and asked me to come Sunday. He said he would personally help me out.

Sunday morning finally arrived, and I was a nervous wreck. I got sick several times before I left home. When I drove to the church, the voices in my head drove me insane. I kept hearing how bad I was, that God hated me and the people there would hate me and hurt me. At the church I sat in my car for a while because I felt like I was going to have a breakdown. Finally I did muster enough courage to walk inside.

Thank God I did. When I went in, I was totally amazed by the love I felt from the people. They welcomed me as if I was family, and when I asked for the pastor by name, they went and got him. The pastor gave me the same awesome sense of feeling loved and welcomed, and he took me in and introduced me to others. I sat by some who gave me their phone numbers.

I didn't hear a lot that day; my mind was pretty closed. The miracle was that I stayed till the end, and when I left, I wanted to come back. No one judged me, no one looked down on me, and everyone greeted me with a smile and hugs. I was totally surprised by it all. That was the changing point for me. I always assumed every church was the same and that I hated all of them. But this church was different. That's what I needed to keep coming back.

Every day of the week became a real battle inside me. Every Saturday night I would get sick and nervous, and every Sunday morning it took all I had to get ready and go. Today I know it was a battle for my very soul, my life. I continued going, and I started asking the pastor a lot of questions about salvation. He always took time to talk with me. He never once condemned or threatened me with hell and damnation.

The week leading up to Easter became a battle and a very bad week for me personally. I had nightmares and got sick. I guess it was Easter morning that I heard a voice inside me, and it wasn't a familiar voice. It wasn't mean or evil, and it didn't mean to hurt me at all. The voice was from Jesus, and He told me that if I didn't accept Him into my life today, that I was going to walk out of worship and never have another chance again. The message was clear and loving. The ball was in my court.

My world went crazy during worship. I could not shut the bad voices up. They were straight from hell. I didn't hear one word of the songs, and I couldn't hear the message, but an amazing thing happened to me at the end. I didn't ask God to help me; He just knew I needed it, and He calmed my spirit.

The pastor showed a clip from the movie *The Passion of the Christ*, and I heard every word. I saw every scene, and I wanted this Jesus more than anything I had ever wanted in my life. On Easter 2006 I admitted I was a sinner, and I asked Jesus to forgive me and save me.

Guess what? Jesus did that and more. I was baptized that summer, and I completed counseling. My life today is blessed. I wake up every day and thank God for my life and for saving me—not just from hell but also from my own hands and the evil that almost destroyed me.

I've become involved in service work at my church because not only is it a calling from Jesus, but it's also a way for me to give back just little of what God has given to me. God has blessed me with an incredible hunger to learn from His Word, and I do, every day. I know that if I am in His Word and doing what He wants me to do, I am growing and can remain useful for His kingdom.

When a visitor walks in my church, I always remember how I felt and what a burden I carried inside me. The way we treat one another can really be a matter of life and death. The motto I remind myself of each day is, "But for the grace of God, there go I."

RECOMMENDED RESOURCES

- *From Darkness to Light: How to Rescue Someone You Love From the Occult* by Jeff Harshbarger (Bridge-Logos, 2004)

- *The Kingdom of the Occult* by Walter Martin, Jill Martin Rische, and Kurt Van Gorden (Thomas Nelson, 2008)

- *Satanism* by Bruce G. Frederickson (Concordia Publishing, 1995)

- *Witchcraft and Satanism* by Walter Martin, CD/audiotape (Walter Martin Ministries, www.waltermartin.com)

- *Unmasking Satan* by Richard Mayhue (Victor Books, 1988)

- *Satanism: Is Your Family Safe?* by Ted Schwarz and Duane Empey (Zondervan, 1988)

Born in Maryland in 1961, Becky Marie Hutchinson remains there with her ninety-one-year-old father and sixteen-year-old nephew. She is an active member of Calvary Chapel of Waldorf.

Chapter 5

THE REALITY OF CHRISTIAN WITCHCRAFT

By Kristine McGuire

T HERE WAS A time in my life when I was a witch, medium, and lead investigator for a ghost-hunting group. For eight years I was deeply involved in the occult. The supernatural became a way of life for me. The crazy part is that up until that time, I was a Christian.

My story begins when I was very young. I was raised in a Christian home. My family went to church every Sunday. When I was six, a friend invited me to vacation Bible school at her church. It was fun. Throughout the week we played games, sang songs, ate cookies, and heard stories about Jesus—how He healed the sick, fed the hungry, and was kind to children. We learned about the crucifixion and how Jesus was raised from the dead. We were told Jesus could be our friend and Savior if we asked Him.

My six-year-old brain made the connection that if I loved God, I needed to make a choice, so I went to my VBS teacher. She sat me down, asked me some questions, and helped me invite Jesus into my heart. It was an honest experience with the Savior and is the day I still say I became a Christian. There was only one tiny wrinkle.

As I was learning to sing "Jesus Loves the Little Children" and "The B-I-B-L-E" every Sunday and Wednesday at church, I also discovered the supernatural. My first encounters were personal. I began sensing "something" watching me in my bedroom as I played with my dolls or games. An invisible person was standing in front of my bedroom closet. I don't know how or why I felt the spirit; I just did. The sensation ran deep into the pit of my stomach, prickling my spine. I simply recognized it—and still do when it happens to this day. I certainly didn't understand it at the time. In fact, it frightened me, so I pretended not to notice.

The strange feelings didn't stop what became a growing interest in spooky things; they may have even fueled my curiosity. Witches and ghosts fascinated me. I wanted to learn the secret things of the universe. My friends and I would try to read one another's thoughts or examine the "lifelines" of the others' outstretched palms.

During slumber parties we would tell ghost stories and play the game "Light as a Feather, Stiff as a Board." Do you remember that game? My friends and I would gather in a circle. The room lights would be turned off. The eerie glow of flashlights, strategically placed at our feet, would provide the only illumination. One girl would volunteer to be in the middle as the rest of us moved in close enough for our shoulders to touch.

We'd extend our hands, touching the girl in the center with two fingers. Closing our eyes, we'd begin the chant: "Light as a feather, stiff as a board."

The words were quiet. We'd say them over and over, rising in pitch and intensity until we intuitively knew to lift the girl as if she were floating. The game is a creepy attempt at levitation, still played by giggling girls intent on scaring one another in the dead of night.

As I grew older, I found books in the school library that fueled my interest in magick. I watched television specials about haunted houses and monsters. My greatest ambition was to become either a Gypsy fortune-teller or a missionary in Africa. Can you say "double-minded"?

In my defense, no one told me there was a problem with my occult-related activities. Nobody told me what the Bible had to say about spirits, witchcraft, or the supernatural. Of course, I wasn't asking any questions either. Most of the adults I remember in those days probably thought such occult interests were harmless, make-believe fun. That attitude hasn't changed much in the past forty years.

As a sixteen-year-old I decided to read the Bible from cover to cover. Talk about an eye opener! I discovered that psychics, talking to the dead, divination, and most everything I was interested in was forbidden by God.

> When you come into the land that the LORD your God is giving you, you shall not learn to follow the abominable practices of those nations. There shall not be found among you anyone who burns his son or his daughter as an offering, anyone who practices divination or tells fortunes or interprets omens, or a sorcerer or a charmer or a medium or a necromancer or one who inquires of the dead, for whoever does these things is an abomination to the LORD. And because of these abominations the LORD your God is driving them out before you.
>
> —DEUTERONOMY 18:9–12, ESV

> And when they say to you, "Inquire of the mediums and the necromancers who chirp and mutter," should not a people inquire of their God? Should they inquire of the dead on behalf of the living?
>
> —ISAIAH 8:19, ESV

In my heart I wanted to please God. So I made the decision to stay away from anything having to do with the occult. But the damage had already been done. In fact, a spiritual tug-of-war began in my life. I loved God. My desire was to serve Him, but I couldn't seem to let go of my interest in psychics, ghosts, or magick.

I stopped reading the horoscopes in magazines, but I couldn't help but be intrigued every time I saw a sign advertising psychic readings. When my school sponsored "Penny Carnivals" (providing games such as "the lollipop tree" or "fish pond" to be enjoyed for a penny), if there was a fortune-teller, I'd plunk myself down in the seat. I didn't play séance games anymore, but I still watched movies and read books about ghosts. And there were the personal experiences.

Demonic Encounter

In 1985 I transferred from the community college I was attending to a small Christian liberal arts college in West Palm Beach, Florida. It was my first time away from home. I loved it! The palm trees and warm ocean breeze seemed so exotic compared to my upbringing in West Michigan. Everything was new and exciting. I confess to feeling homesick when autumn came and the trees were still green. I phoned my mother, asking her to send me a box of leaves from the trees in our yard. She didn't.

I made good friends in college. I was sharing an apartment-style dorm with three other young women. The four girls living next door to us were fun. We'd do homework together or hang out on the front walkway to share a bit of school gossip. One of the girls and I hit it off. We'd chat or go for long walks near the Intracoastal Waterway. She was becoming a trusted friend.

When a four-day weekend approached, my roommates went to their respective homes. But because I lived so far away, I was scheduled to remain on campus until winter break the following month. Truthfully, I was looking forward to having the place to myself for a few days. I'd spent several weekends alone in the dorm, so it was no big deal.

The first two days were peaceful. I met my neighbor for lunch and dinner in the nearly deserted cafeteria. The friend who'd introduced me to the school was from my home church in Michigan. She lived in a dorm across campus as a resident advisor. I knew she was staying as well. Friday night turned out to be kind of dull with most of the students away. I watched a little television in the Student Center before walking back to my dorm and going to bed.

I awoke in the early-morning hours. The street lamp was casting its usual soft glow through the blinds on my window. The pavement below rumbled with the hum of the 2:00 a.m. traffic. I listened to the ambient noises in my room, trying to discern what had disturbed my sleep. I felt an oppressive heaviness in the air above me.

And then I heard it. Words whispered but harsh in my ear: "*Get out!*"

My feet hit the ground running. Terrified, I bolted from my room, which was in the back section of the apartment, through the front room to the door. My fingers scrambled for the keys, which were hanging on a small rack beside the door. I twisted the small lock on the handle to unlock the door before yanking it open. I barely remembered to shut and lock the door behind me.

In T-shirt and shorts, I fled barefoot across the campus. I didn't go to my neighbor or my own resident advisor in the apartment below mine. In blind panic I chose the friend who was as far from my dorm as possible. Maybe because she represented a connection with home? I honestly don't know.

I banged on the door of my friend's dorm until someone opened it. The girls looked at me. Seeing the state I was in, one girl ushered me into the front hall as another went to roust my friend out of bed. I must have looked the way I felt because my friend took me by the arm and led me to her room. She sat beside me on the bed as I explained what happened and begged to sleep on her floor. She stood and walked to a nearby closet, retrieving an extra blanket and pillow. Once I was settled on a space on the floor, my friend prayed for me. She was convinced I'd had a vivid nightmare.

The next day, after borrowing a pair of flip-flops, I wandered back across campus to my dorm. I took a deep breath, settling my nerves, before inserting the key in the lock and opening the door. I walked through the apartment to my room. The atmosphere seemed oppressive and wrong. Fear began welling within me. I took the time to get dressed but left as quickly as possible.

I sought out my neighbor. Moments after knocking on her door, she opened it and invited me in with a cheerful smile. We sat on her couch, chatting about nothing until I got up the nerve to share my story. She listened with interest.

"This isn't the first time," I explained. I told her about being able to sense spirits from childhood. I related an episode from when I was sixteen. One night I'd gotten into bed and was just lying down when I felt afraid. I heard loud breathing near my ear, and the mattress dipped behind my back as if someone had sat down on the bed.

"What did you do?" she asked.

"Freaked out. Told my mom. She called our pastor, and he came a few days later," I replied. "He prayed in the room. Told the demon it had to leave in Jesus's name. Never bothered me again."

My neighbor nodded thoughtfully.

"I believe in spirits and stuff."

"Yeah?" I inquired. "Would you pray in my room with me?"

"Sure."

Getting up from the couch we marched out onto the walkway bordering our rooms. We walked the few steps from her door to mine. I unlocked the door, and we moved through the front room to mine. We took turns, agreeing in prayer that whatever spirit had invaded my dorm had to leave in Jesus's name. When we finished we looked at each other.

"It feels different in here," my neighbor remarked. "Better."

"Definitely," I agreed.

STRIVING FOR PERFECTION

You would think that having been aware of the spiritual realm my whole life, repeatedly witnessing and participating in spiritual warfare, I would have had more sense as I got older. But the lure of the supernatural, paranormal, and the occult would draw me inch by inch.

When I graduated from college, married a Christian man, and

began a family, I became earnest in finding ways to please God. I wanted to be the perfect wife and mother. My husband and I came from broken homes, so I was determined to have the perfect Christian marriage. I volunteered at church, prayed an hour a day, and read my Bible faithfully.

There is no such thing as a perfect Christian, but that didn't stop me from trying to become one. As life intervened with hard choices, financial difficulty, and the pressure of being a wife and mother, disappointment festered within me. My husband and I fought over how to raise our daughters, what it meant to be a family, and how to make our marriage work.

I wanted him to be the spiritual leader of our home, but he didn't seem interested in the job. I felt responsible for everything. My husband seemed to believe his task was to provide income and little else. My frustration became anger. I thought if I did all the right things, God would respond with blessings.

As my husband and I struggled through emotional and spiritual issues, it seemed as though God had abandoned me. My faith became nonexistent. My spiritual life was nothing but dry religion. I was thirsty for anything that could provide relief.

In 1999 I turned to witchcraft for answers. My first step was to explore a fast-growing religion known as Wicca. Wicca is an earth-centered goddess religion that uses ritual and magick. I worked as a Christian preschool teacher and attended church with my family to keep up the pretense.

In secret I learned about the mystical correspondences of gemstones, plants, colors, and other items. Over the course of a year I studied the phases of the moon as it waxed and waned. I learned how to meditate using Eastern religious techniques. I discovered my personal energy through visualization. One exercise included creating a ball of energy in my right hand. I would then toss the energy ball into the air, catching it with my left hand. I visualized the glow the energy ball emitted. I felt the shape of it in my hand.

I observed full moon rituals called esbats. I reached out with my thoughts to goddesses such as Artemis, Brighid, Aphrodite, and others. The goddess welcomed me with visions and dreams. She guided me in making decisions. In one such instance I was encouraged to leave my husband.

My visions were always intense. In this one I was running through a forest chasing a stag. A long bow was in my hand, a quiver of arrows strapped across my back. Artemis ran beside me. When the stag came to rest in front of a tree, Artemis commanded me to shoot it. I obeyed. The arrow pierced the animal. As the stag fell, it transformed into the image of my husband. When I came to myself, I was distraught but realized my marriage was dead. Not long after the vision I discovered my husband was having an online affair with another woman. My course was set. I left my husband a month later, gratified that the goddess had led me toward that conclusion with the warning vision. I felt empowered and justified.

Three years would pass before I moved from goddess worship to what is known as traditional witchcraft. What's interesting is how the Holy Spirit was reaching out to me from the beginning of my occult explorations. God was prodding and convicting me of my sin. This led me to years of waffling between witchcraft and Christianity. I would spend months immersed in activities such as using a pendulum to divine the future or reading tarot cards. I spent hours reading books on how to increase psychic abilities. I looked for ways to communicate with spirits through becoming a medium and ghost hunting.

But then the doubts would stir in my thoughts. What if everything I'd learned in the Bible was true? How would my children be affected by my occult activities? Plagued with doubt, I would throw away my "stuff." The small iron cauldron used for incense. The assorted gemstones hand-picked by the energy I sensed within them. The handcrafted wand or various candles used for spellcraft. I'd throw them away or give them to other witches I knew.

I wanted to be sincere in those decisions. I wanted to serve God with my whole heart. But in the end the accoutrements of the Craft would find their way back into my possession. I'd buy a new set of tarot cards. My occult books would be replaced.

Eventually I grew tired of it all. I wanted my Christian beliefs without restrictions. I wanted magick without feeling judged. Above all I wanted to end the relentless feelings of guilt. I decided to create a spiritual path that would incorporate the best of both worlds. I began practicing Christian witchcraft.

I know what you're thinking right about now. "Hang on, back the truck up. Christian witchcraft? Impossible!" You think so? Friend, we live in a world that has declared absolute truth to be "offensive." People have created a mantra out of the phrase "I'm spiritual but not religious." The Bible holds little to no authority in many of our churches today, let alone in individual lives. The fear of God is absent from our society. There is nothing that prevents people from practicing witchcraft and being completely comfortable in calling themselves a Christian while doing so.

So how is it possible to be a Christian and a witch? I can speak only for myself, but I had a deconstructionist view of the Bible. This means I left Scripture open to my own interpretation or disregarded what I believed pertained to its time period or particular audience. I examined the definition of individual words and created meaning to support my position.

For instance, Exodus 22:18 (NLT) says, "You must not allow a sorceress to live." The original Hebrew word translated "sorceress" is *m'khashepah.* The root word, *kashaph,* is translated "to whisper" (as in a spell, sorcery, or enchantment to harm others). As a witch I believed magick was neutral, with *the intention of the practitioner* being the key. I chose to practice magick that benefited my life and family. Therefore the judgment against a sorceress (or witch) did not apply to me. See how that works?

As a Christian witch I incorporated my faith and church symbolism I liked into the Craft. I worshipped Father, Son, and Holy (Mother/Sophia) Spirit. When I cast a sacred circle for ritual or spellcraft, I invited angels to join me as guardians of north, south, east, and west. I used passages from the Book of Psalms for incantations. I believed God was above all things *and in* all things—plants, trees, earth, animals. Witchcraft became the lens through which I viewed the world and expressed my beliefs as a Christian.

Christian witchcraft is not only possible, but it is also a growing phenomenon. More people are practicing spirituality without restrictions, so they glean whatever beliefs appeal to them and mash them together.

The problem is that people tend to get caught up in the stereotypes attached to certain words such as *witchcraft* or *witch*. While there are those who specifically claim Christian witchcraft as their spiritual path (as I did) and call themselves witches, there are plenty of people who are in fact practicing "the Craft." They are not necessarily using those terms, but they are incorporating such things as candle meditation, chakras, or divination into their religious practice. They may call themselves "mystical Christians" or describe their beliefs in some other way, but they are practicing a form of witchcraft all the same.

Witchcraft is not a religion. It is spiritual. It is a way of life and a worldview. This is why it's important to understand that quoting Scripture and telling a Christian witch (or anyone in the occult for that matter) they are "wrong, wrong, wrong" will fall on *deaf ears*. They don't care what the Bible says. It holds no authority in their lives whatsoever. Frustrating, isn't it?

In the end it was evidence caught during a ghost hunt that brought me up short. I came face-to-face with the truth about the spirits I'd been communicating with daily and that empowered all I ever did as a witch. The Holy Spirit pulled the veil of (self) deception from my eyes.

For the first time in eight years I read the Bible without a personal agenda. I wanted to (re)discover the truth about the occult, salvation, and who Jesus is. I realized it was time to make a choice after reading Matthew 6:22–23: "The eye is the lamp of the body. If your eyes are good, your whole body will be full of light. But if your eyes are bad, your whole body will be full of darkness. If then the light within you is darkness, how great is that darkness!"

Did I want to serve God or stubbornly follow my own path into spiritual destruction? In that moment I got down on my face repenting before God of all occult-related activity. I renounced every demonic spirit I'd invited into my life and home. I rededicated my life to Christ and have been serving Him ever since.

I believe it's important to approach people deceived by the enemy with grace and love. Be a friend first. Get to know the person. Don't be afraid to ask them about their beliefs. If they grew up with traditional church teaching, ask them what they have a difficult time accepting or understanding. Tell them your own story—especially if you've ever doubted your own faith.

Be a living witness to people. Explain how God's infinite love and mercy are so much bigger than we can possibly comprehend. As you establish a relationship with a person involved in the occult, let the Holy Spirit guide you in sharing how the truth really does set us free. Do not compromise on the issue of sin, but remember Paul's example:

> Even though I am a free man with no master, I have become a slave to all people to bring many to Christ. When I was with the Jews, I lived like a Jew to bring the Jews to Christ. When I was with those who follow the Jewish law, I too lived under that law. Even though I am not subject to the law, I did this so I could bring to Christ those who are under the law. When I am with the Gentiles who do not follow the Jewish law, I too live apart from that law so I can bring them to Christ. But I do not ignore the law of God; I obey the law of Christ.
>
> When I am with those who are weak, I share their weakness, for I want to bring the weak to Christ. Yes, I try to find common ground with everyone, doing everything I can to save some. I do everything to spread the Good News and share in its blessings.
>
> —1 Corinthians 9:19–23, NLT

Witchcraft and mysticism have been gaining acceptance in our society over the past forty years. The church has been hiding its face as roots of disobedience and idolatry have taken hold in every corner. Today there is a staggering number of people who call themselves Christian but have no idea what the Bible says. Young people are leaving church as they graduate from high school without looking back. Goddess worship in the form of "feminist spirituality," Eastern meditation, and mystical encounters are replacing Scripture as the authority upon which some Christians are basing their spiritual future. My question is this: What are you going to do about it?

QUICK FACTS ABOUT GODDESS WORSHIP, WITCHCRAFT, AND WICCA

• Pagans define witchcraft as a practice centered around the casting of spells and working of magick; it may involve the worship of individual deities (polytheism).

• Wicca is a religion focused on the worship of the Lord and Lady, and other goddesses and gods; it is based on nature magick and Hindu/New Age thought.

• Neopaganism is the worship of ancient pagan deities; it is an umbrella term for all pagan beliefs, such as goddess worship, witchcraft, Wicca, druidism, shamanism, and other non-Christian belief systems.

• Neopagan beliefs can be animistic (the view that all objects, including the universe, have a soul), pantheistic (the belief that the divine is present within the life of all things), panenthestic (the view that the divine is in all and greater than all), or all three.

• Neopaganism views the biblical God as one of many gods or as an aspect of the one universal goddess/god. Some neopagans believe Jesus is simply a wise man and possibly even a witch.[1]

• Neopagans claim there is no such thing as "evil" or original sin; reincarnation replaces salvation.[2]

THE TRUTH ABOUT WITCHES, WICCANS, AND PAGANS

I always find it interesting how unaware Christians in general are when it comes to the occult. I'm reminded of this when speaking to churches. While sharing my testimony, I have asked how many people know about or had heard of Wicca or paganism. I would receive raised eyebrows or blank stares as my answer. Seriously. You could hear crickets chirp two states away because of the awkward silence.

In fact, this has happened so often I no longer bother asking the question. As soon as the word *Wicca* escapes my lips, I offer an abbreviated definition. By doing so, I'm relatively certain listeners will understand what I'm referring to. I do the same thing when we get to the ghost hunting.

I've also discovered that those who do know about Wicca, paganism, or witchcraft often have a mistaken view of the people involved. The problem is that these perceptions of witches, Wiccans, or pagans confuse Christians and hurt Wiccans, witches, or pagans. And they make it difficult to share the gospel with people who need to hear it.

So what is the truth about witches, Wiccans, and pagans? Wicca is considered to be one of the fastest-growing religions in America, particularly among high school- and college-age women, a large majority of whom come from traditional church backgrounds.

Wicca, an earth-based goddess religion that incorporates ritual and magick, is filled with people who have found a connection with the universe through the myths of the ancient gods and goddesses. The holiday calendar they follow and the rituals they perform are reimagined from ancient paganism. Wiccans are "save the planet" kind of people.

Like most people, Wiccans (and other pagans) are looking for deeper meaning in their lives. They believe its fine to "do what thou wilt," as long as no one is harmed. They don't believe in Satan, sin, or the need to be forgiven.

Wiccans, witches, and pagans revere nature. God/dess (or universal energy) is in everything and everyone. Some Wiccans and pagans do not incorporate magick or spellcraft into their spiritual path. Wiccans, witches, and pagans do embrace various occult practices, including divination and spirit communication.

Wicca and other forms of paganism are defined as religions. Witchcraft can best be understood as a way of life or worldview—a worldview tempered by the witch's personal ethics and aligned to his or her personal religious or spiritual beliefs.

All witches practice magick. They believe in the energy and cycles of the earth, universe, and spirit within themselves. Witches use spellcraft and the natural world (plants, herbs, stones, and crystals) to harness that spiritual energy to affect changes or outcomes they desire.

I've offered a very brief overview of complex religious and spiritual belief systems. Wiccans, witches, and pagans believe the deity or power they experience is good and helpful to their lives. This is important for Christians to acknowledge and respect—because underneath the witchcraft and mysticism is a human being whom God loves.

As Christians we understand the true nature of what's empowering Wicca, witchcraft, and the occult. The Bible tells us in Ephesians 6:12, 2 Corinthians 4:4, Isaiah 44:6–20, 1 Timothy 4:1, and Acts 16:16–18 that all works of the occult and witchcraft are, in fact, demonic. The gods and goddesses of Wicca, paganism, and witchcraft are deceptive spirits masquerading as beings of light. They lure people away from God's revealed plan of salvation through Jesus Christ.

As Christians we are called to share the gospel with everyone, regardless of where they have been or what they've done. Sadly, I've spoken with Christians who are afraid to talk with witches or Wiccans. Some believe people involved in the occult are not worth the risk. They fear being influenced by demonic spirits themselves, or they think individuals involved in witchcraft or paganism are too strongly influenced by the enemy. We have no need to be afraid. As disciples of Jesus Christ, we submit ourselves to God. We are able to claim the authority of Jesus's name. What have we to fear with God on our side?

As Christians we should be extending the hand of friendship to those around us—including Wiccans, witches, and pagans. After all, to be Jesus's disciple means to follow His model. Why don't we invite people to have a calm dialogue with us? Let's listen to them and find out what attracted them to paganism or Wicca in the first place. Then we can share what Jesus Christ has done in our own lives and the hope He has given us. We can follow Paul's example in Athens by persuading people with the truth and never compromising on sin (Acts 17:15–34). We can be a witness through our actions as well as our words.

The truth about witches, Wiccans, and pagans is that they are no different than any other person on this planet. God loves them, and so should we.[3]

RECOMMENDED RESOURCES

To learn more about the deceptive nature of Wicca, witchcraft, and paganism, and how they veer from the truth of God's Word, I recommend the following resources:

- *Escaping the Cauldron* by Kristine McGuire (Charisma House, 2012)

- *Goddess Worship, Witchcraft and Neo-Paganism* by Craig S. Hawkins (Zondervan, 1998)

- *Evil and Human Suffering*, CD/ audiotape by Walter Martin (Walter Martin Ministries, www .waltermartin.com)

- *Jesus: God, Man or Myth?* CD/ audiotape by Walter Martin (Walter Martin Ministries, www .waltermartin.com)

- *Wicca's Charm* by Catherine Edwards Saunders (Shaw Publishing, 2005)

- *The Kingdom of the Occult* by Walter Martin, Jill Rische, and Kurt Van Gorden (Thomas Nelson, 2008)

Kristine McGuire (www.kristinemcguire.com) is a Christian wife and mother, working in ministry with her husband, Thom McGuire. She has written a book about her experiences as a Christian witch called Escaping the Cauldron *and is available as a speaker for youth, women's, and church events.*

Chapter 6

FROM SPIRITUALISM TO CHRIST

By Laura Maxwell

The Death of a Medium

A mother who muttered and spoke with the dead,
With ease predicting future events
Dreams and visions played out in her head,
To development séances, she gladly went.
For *this* destiny was I born?
Events unexplained that brought a thrill.
A life for the occult was being formed,
Strange sights drew me in deeper still.
From astral projection to yoga and zen,
Sketching ghosts—the psychic arts,
Crystals and chakras, trance and T.M.,
Our home became haunted. Fear seized our hearts.
Then mother became more and more ill,
Dangerous accidents—terror by night.
Spirits controlling against her will,
Levitating furniture, a common sight.
Psychics and mediums who tried their best,
To rid our home of unwelcome guests.
No help from gods of wood or stone,
Mum and I lost in our cursed home.

Part Two

Afraid to stay in, afraid to go out,
Wherever she went, they would follow.
Their evil voices would mock and shout,
Cars halt, as spirits threw her across the road.
Events became more absurd,

I feared what would befall my mum.
Trapped in an unseen world,
For her, this meant the end had come.
Hell's final surge. The gates opened wide,
Spirits assailed her like a tide,
Mum's last action—suicide.
My screams of horror echoed that night,
I found a Bible, searching for Light.
Praying, "Who is the true God? Please reveal.
Jesus Christ, is He Savior of all?"
His Word showed me Jesus forgives and heals,
"Ghosts" screamed—fled the house when *His Name* I called,
Peace flooded my soul like a waterfall.
I learned to trust Him. His Love cast out fears.
Joy in His Presence. Worship sublime.
A *new* church family I can call mine.
Christ lovingly saved me from Satan's snare.
Too late now, for Mum to pray,
If still alive what would she say?
"Don't dabble in New Age,
Please! Not even a spell.
Why sign your life over to a living hell?"

—Based on true events.
Dedicated in loving memory of my mother

I have a family history of spiritualism and New Age involvement on my mother's side. One of my mother's uncles was a Freemason and a head medium at his spiritualist church in Scotland. My mother experienced psychic phenomena beginning in her childhood, though she did not seriously begin to pursue spiritualism until later.

By the time I began secondary school, my mom felt ready to experiment with the occult. One day, while walking her dogs in the park, a local spiritualist medium approached my mother, telling her he saw potential in her to develop as a medium. He invited her to a spiritualist church in Glasgow.

Very quickly Mum became engrossed by the supernatural. As a

new member of the spiritualist church, she attended Sunday services, midweek psychic development groups, and transcendental meditation and yoga classes. She shared everything she learned with me at home, and I also became fascinated.

The desire of my mother's heart was to train to one day become a medium. The other mediums in her church encouraged this, inviting her to join an open circle to learn how to meditate and develop in the area of channeling the spirits of the deceased. Mum was keen to develop her abilities of clairvoyance, which is the seeing of spirits; clairaudience, or hearing voices of spirits; and clairsentience, which is sensing the presence of spirits.

My mother would book a private reading, also known as a private sitting, with a resident or visiting medium. These were private appointments, and the mediums were always paid for them. After the reading Mum would buy a recording of the session, and we'd both listen to it later that day. It amazed me that a session lasting thirty minutes could contain so much clear communication from spirits.

The mediums relayed minute details about our lives, often giving precise names, places, and dates. It was obvious they weren't charlatans who used trickery or fell upon the correct names by sheer chance. Mediums accurately described the physical appearance and personalities of our dead relatives and even repeated the common phrases of the deceased as they apparently conversed with them.

When old enough to attend, I also joined the spiritualist church and attended weekly. As a young teenager I also developed a hunger for spiritualism. I became increasingly fascinated by psychic readings and healing, rebirthing, crystal healing, meditation, hypnosis, and the like. We read books on astrology, telepathy, and astral projection, and sampled many alternative-healing therapies.

My mother and I were on a constant search for more mystical books. We devoured titles on extrasensory perception (ESP), reincarnation, opening the *chakras* ("wheels" of energy), and so on. It became almost an addiction. We read spiritualist journals and papers such as *The Psychic News,* as well as books with apparent communications from dead spirits, or teachings by ascended masters, White Eagle, and others. We listened in fascination to friends' reports of events at the Findhorn New Age center in Scotland and hoped to travel the few hours' journey to visit there someday.

Attending New Age centers and psychic fairs across Glasgow, we absorbed as much information as we could to aid in our spiritual enlightenment. With our passion for environmental and conservation concerns, social justice, and international peace, we gladly participated in attempts to heal people and animals through either contact or distant forms of psychic healing.

When I had an appointment with a visiting medium for my first private reading, I was told that my dead sister and grandmother were in the room with us. At first I thought the medium had made a mistake, as I didn't have a sister. The medium insisted. Mum later confessed that she had never told me she had lost a baby.

Also, my grandmother died when I was very young, so I couldn't remember what she looked like. Later that day my mother also confirmed that the description of Gran given by the medium was accurate. Many instances like these proved to me that mediums were genuine and not charlatans using guesswork or suggestion.

GOING DEEPER

Mediums predicted I'd become a psychic artist, drawing portraits of the dead and selling them to spiritualists or the bereaved relative. I bought a book by a well-known English psychic artist to learn more. They also encouraged me to start psychic or Kirlian photography, which uses infrared film to catch images of spirits and ectoplasm.

I didn't pursue either of these practices deeply as I was too busy at school and then later attending college, but I planned to pursue them seriously later. Meanwhile Mum was developing in automatic writing, where spirits took over her hand and wrote sacred texts through her. She wouldn't even need to concentrate on what she was writing. It flowed out of her hand without any conscious effort on her part, as the spirits controlled and used her as their vessel of communication.

It all seemed wonderful, until I reached my late teens/early twenties. Over the next ten years we'd often hear of mediums who could no longer control when spirits spoke to or through them. Many mediums had nervous breakdowns or attacked people, claiming their spirit guides had forced them to; several mediums were admitted to psychiatric wards. We even heard reports of "poltergeist" activity.

At first we accepted explanations that mischievous or obnoxious spirits could sometimes come through, and this was viewed as a potential hazard of the job. But when it began to happen to us, it became difficult to tolerate and almost impossible to function properly. Before, the spirits appeared only when Mum invited them, but they now demanded more of her time. They spoke to Mum constantly, depriving her of sleep, attacking her physically, clapping loudly from within wardrobes, and slamming all the doors.

By then we began to suffer psychological effects from the spiritual problems, as well as feelings of evil foreboding, sleep paralysis, and night terrors. Mum and I would feel spirit hands or heavy weights and presences pushing down on our bodies. We would sometimes feel invisible hands attempting to choke and strangle us. Even then we heard this could be common for some people in spiritualism. Through the years our friends, the other psychics and mediums, kindly tried to help but failed to free our home from spirits. I've since spoken to and heard of countless others who also experienced such attacks when dabbling in spiritualism or New Age.

Some Christians may read this and initially doubt that spirits can be physically felt. I can't pretend to understand the physics involved, but the Bible does refer to the fact that spirits and angels do have a type of body, although different in substance to ours. In the Bible we see that angels can struggle and fight with demonic spirits, suggesting they aren't just wisps but have a substance. The Angel of the Lord wrestled with Jacob all night, leaving him with a limp (Gen. 32:24–31).

Furthermore, Acts 12:7 says, "Suddenly an angel of the Lord appeared and a light shone in the cell. He struck Peter on the side and woke him up. 'Quick, get up!' he said, and the chains fell off Peter's wrists." If God's angels can strike a human with physical force, so can Satan's angels. Rather than assuming someone has a vivid imagination when they report "poltergeist activity," we should pray and, with Christ's wisdom, discern what is going on.

Similarly, some Christians may doubt whether spirits can enter our level of atmosphere. As the Bible says in Ephesians 6:12: "We are not fighting against humans. We are fighting against forces and authorities and against rulers of darkness and powers in the spiritual world" (CEV). And we read in 1 Peter 5:8, "Be self-controlled and alert. Your enemy the devil prowls around like a roaring lion looking for someone to devour." If Satan, being the prince of the air, can move in our atmosphere, so can his demonic servants.

Although Mum and I were members of one spiritualist church, we often visited two other spiritualist churches too. At these three churches (including *Christian* spiritualist churches), we heard more rumors from members and visitors that sometimes mediums' homes could become "haunted," or spirit-possessed to be more accurate.

These spiritualists also told us of mediums whose once-faithful, long-term "spirit guides" turned on them for no apparent reason, keeping them awake at night. Some experienced tangible demonic activity. For example, spirits would throw furniture around the room or cause the electrical appliances to operate even though they were not switched on or plugged into a power source. You would think we'd see these warning signs as a prompt to withdraw from spiritualism, but like most spiritualists, we didn't interpret it that way. Instead we accepted, as many did, that periodic spiritual assaults, or "psychic warfare," was just an occupational hazard to be expected on occasion.

The head mediums showed concern for the victimized spiritualists and could sometimes help prevent these attacks, but often they were limited or powerless in totally stopping such events. As I stated previously, in time we began to hear of more individuals who were admitted to psychiatric wards because they'd become highly stressed, disoriented, and a danger to themselves and others. We heard of a few mediums who even attacked people, saying their spirit guides took total control over them, forcing them to hurt others.

Similar traumatic incidents continued to happen to us. We were subjected to more poltergeist activity. We both continued to be physically attacked by the spirits. Mum was more victimized than I was. She was even thrown around inside the house and often forced into trances against her will.

On one of the occasions when the spirits forced her into a trance, she was frying food. When she came out of trance, the kitchen was consumed by fire. I arrived home after the firefighters had extinguished it, just before it spread to other rooms. We all realized that Mum and our dogs and cats could have been injured or killed. One afternoon when we were out, Mum's elderly aunt (who had also visited spiritualist churches) came to Mum's house to feed our dogs and cats. Although alone in Mum's house, our aunt felt invisible hands grab her and throw her down our stairs. Her wrist was broken.

Another day while approaching a shopping area, I watched in horror as Mum was lifted from the ground and catapulted from the pavement, landing on the hood of a slowly passing car. On other occasions while shopping, she was lifted from the street and thrown onto the road in front of passing cars.

▰ QUICK FACTS ABOUT SPIRITUALISM

Some official writings of spiritualism claim compatibility with Christianity. *The A.B.C. of Spiritualism* claims "the real beginning of Christianity, its motive power, its great impetus, came—not from the birth or death of Jesus—but from Pentecost, the greatest séance in history."[1] Nothing could be further from the truth. Here are the facts:

• Spiritualism is not based on the Bible.

• Spiritualists believe in the divinity of Jesus—because they believe that as children of God everyone is divine.

• Spiritualism does not recognize Jesus as one person of the Trinity, coequal with the Father and divine in a sense in which divinity is unattainable by other men. Spiritualism accepts Jesus as one of many savior christs, who at different times have come into the world to lighten its darkness.

• Spiritualism does not recognize special value and efficacy in the death of Jesus in saving men.

• Spiritualists believe Jesus was a great mediator or medium.

• Spiritualists do not believe in any version of a great white throne or lake of fire.[2]

DEADLY ENCOUNTERS

Mum and I were at the end of our ropes. We couldn't go on living that way. We decided to withdraw from spiritualism and told our spirit guides to leave. It was actually when we attempted to leave spiritualism that the attacks grew far worse. To our shock the spirits laughed and insulted us. They physically attacked us. This was perplexing, as they had provided guidance and kindness for many years. It became obvious they'd deceived us, pretending to be benevolent when in reality they were wicked all along.

The biggest shock, however, came when even our dead relatives turned against us. They mocked and hit us. The spirits warned we couldn't leave the occult, as we had unknowingly given them control from the first day we invited them into our lives. I've since heard of and read of such occurrences in Christian books by former spiritualists, such as *Beware the Devil* by English-born former medium Robert Lee.

We had also heard rumors of a few mediums who had progressed to Satanism. We'd been told that sometimes Satanists secretly infiltrate spiritualist churches to scout for new members. They could sense the mediums with potential to become Satanists. Although we believed this to be rare, it was disconcerting nonetheless.

When people had a negative experience with a bad spirit, mediums kindly explained a "lower-level spirit" had managed to get through. Mediums emphasized that usually spirit guides should manage to protect spiritualists from this. Mediums *always* told Mum and me that we had "good vibes and energies" and that *our* spirit guides and relatives were genuine and not mischievous imposters. However, the mediums would say if a person had low morals or "bad vibes" that attracted a low-level, violent spirit, it wasn't easy to help that person or to prevent the spirits from attacking them. Often there was even the suggestion that the person had somehow deserved such spiritual abuse.

Mediums couldn't, therefore, explain why our trustworthy spirit friends suddenly became obnoxious and violent toward us. It wasn't a case of like attracts like, as the mediums we knew explained we had good spirit guides and that Mum and I had no negative energies or bad karma. The mediums said we *didn't* have less-evolved guides and that we had not signed up for this trouble in a prior life.

So if the usual spiritualist explanations given for such situations didn't explain what we were experiencing, what did? The only answer was that spiritualism itself was highly dangerous and questionable in its very origins and claims.

Eventually friends who were New Agers or spiritualists all abandoned us, as they knew mediums had failed to clear our house of "bad" spirits. Maybe they were embarrassed or afraid. They were all very nice folks, and I suppose it must have been very confusing and frightening for them.

When I became a Christian, I forgave them for deserting us.

They acted in ignorance and had no idea what was truly going on, so there was no reason for me to be bitter or hold grudges against them. On the contrary, I desperately wanted them to see the demonic deception at work in it all and to become Christians too, finding peace and love in Christ.

Most of the spiritualists we met were kind, genuine, helpful folks with good motives. They weren't evil or nasty, as some ill-informed people assume. I rarely met a medium I disliked. Let me emphasize that I haven't an axe to grind with any psychic; it's the evil spirits at work in those individuals that I dislike.

My mother's "spirit guides" continued to come through her almost twenty-four hours a day against her will. They told her to commit murders. Accusing locals of heinous crimes, they insisted Mum would be working for God by killing them! Police were involved due to Mum's threatening letters to locals. She even told me she would have to kill my dad, as spirits told her he was the devil. By now my parents had divorced, and Dad wasn't aware of the full extent of our problems. He never had approved of Mum introducing me to spiritualism.

We desperately tried to break away from spiritualism. One night Mum was attacked all night and saw a large evil eye on her bedroom wall. She called it "the all-seeing eye." She saw snakes on her bed. A being appeared. He was so evil and threatening, she thought it was Satan. The next morning she told me it only disappeared when she shouted Jesus Christ repeatedly. She told me it was the worst night of her entire life.

The spirit who had impersonated my "dead sister" had visited me for years, often stroking my hair at night. But now, because we were trying to leave spiritualism, when the entity visited me, it would wrap its hands around my throat, trying to strangle me. It would leave me choking and coughing, causing the bed to move with the struggle.

Mum and I tried to prevent these constant attacks by "cleansing our auras," "closing our chakras," and so on. We called on spirit guides that we believed were more evolved to come and help us. We copied lists of gods from encyclopedias of religion. We called on these many different gods to help us, including Buddhist and Hindu gods. Not one of those gods could take control of it or help us in any way. Indeed, the more gods we called on, the worse our situation became.

This continued for years. While studying art at college I met and fell in love with the loving and supportive man I was to marry. Even after we moved into our own home and had our wonderful baby boy, Mum was still experiencing these spiritual attacks. I was too, but to a much lesser extent. My husband wasn't interested in pursuing spiritualism and was obviously concerned about the situation with Mum and myself. When our child began preschool, I enrolled in a psychology honors degree. During my second year at university, Mum's health deteriorated, and her "spirit guides" continued to threaten to use her to kill people.

Mum visited her doctor for tranquilizers or sleeping pills, explaining her situation. But Mum's doctor couldn't accept her accounts of poltergeist activity and, diagnosing her as a schizophrenic, the doctor made arrangements to detain my mother in a psychiatric hospital.

This was a very traumatic time for our family but particularly for my mother and myself. In the first few weeks Mum took her anger out on me, blaming me for not being able to persuade the psychiatrist it was a spiritual problem. But the truth was, whether spiritual or not, Mum's mental health was now affected, and her safety and the safety of others were seriously jeopardized.

We did remember that even mediums we had known who were psychiatric nurses said they heard the same voices some of their patients were hearing. They had said some patients weren't ill but just had problems of spirit harassment.

A Christian Encounter

By now I'd been involved in spiritualism for around ten to fifteen years. I had confided in a new friend I'd met in a psychology tutorial. She was a Christian and invited me to her Pentecostal church, explaining that other psychics who had experienced similar tragedies were set free from spiritual attacks only when they accepted Jesus Christ as their Savior. These people were now members of her church.

She told me that a visiting preacher was coming, and, as he was prophetic, he'd most likely give prophecies. She said I was welcome to go with her to church and check it out. As a spiritualist, the idea of prophecy attracted me right away! If a prophetic preacher wasn't due to visit, I doubt I'd have gone, as I thought all Christian churches were boring and devoid of all spirituality.

At that meeting fifteen years ago the preacher prophesied to me things that had taken place in recent years. Although I didn't convert to Christianity that night, I began to consider the possibility that Christianity was the truth. As New Agers are open-minded, I then realized I had to at least consider the gospel and consider that maybe Christ was indeed the only way to God.

In the past I'd argued that the New Age and spiritualism were the true originals, as they were ancient faiths, founded before the New Testament and birth of Christianity. But I now heard that Christianity stemmed from the Old Testament, which, even according to archaeological and historical evidence, was written fifteen hundred to two thousand years before Christ. If you follow Jesus's genealogy back to Genesis 1:26, where we see Christ was with God the Father before and during Creation, it actually makes Christ *older* than the ancient religions. It was a surprise to consider that Christ existed before paganism and spiritualism began! This was an amazing revelation for a spiritualist!

Much to my surprise I found that the Pentecostal church did not portray dead religious traditions. Instead it was lively, loving, and fun. I was delighted to learn that members were trained by the Holy Spirit to prophesy about people's future, that individuals were physically healed, and other miracles, signs, and wonders occurred. Actually, in a couple of years I saw more peopled healed in Pentecostal churches than I ever saw in over ten years at spiritualist churches!

It made complete sense when Christians explained that it's impossible for dead souls to return to talk with us, as they remain in heaven or hell for eternity. Just before I became a Christian or had read the biblical warnings against the occult, I slowly yet instinctively began to realize what had happened. It began to cross my mind that the spirits at spiritualist meetings were *all* evil imposters. The missing pieces of the jigsaw were beginning to fit into place. When our dead relatives and spirit guides began to attack Mum and me, it indicated they were fakes and had deceived us. They were merely impersonating our loved ones.

When my university friend took me to her Pentecostal church, I was overwhelmed at the happy and loving atmosphere. They were so welcoming and friendly. I totally loved hearing people pray or sing in tongues. I wished all the spiritualists I knew could hear it too! The preacher taught on the storms of life and how you'd be safe if you had Jesus in your boat with you. It caused me to think of my poor mother still stuck in the psychiatric hospital.

The meeting at the Pentecostal church gave me food for thought, although I wasn't yet convinced. One minute it made complete sense to me when Christians explained it's impossible for dead souls to return to talk with us. But the next minute I'd doubt it again! My whole way of thinking and all my mind-sets were thrown into question. I wondered if I was having an identity crisis.

That night when I went home I had a dreadful migraine headache, and I felt the spirits were angry at me for attending a Christian church. Funnily enough, earlier that day I had packed old books into a bag to take to a charity shop. As I opened the door and stepped into our flat, I saw a Bible at the top of the bag where I'd placed it earlier!

It caught my eye, and I decided that, having just returned from a Christian meeting, I should pray and read it. I was quite confused, frightened, and upset. The idea that spiritualism wasn't what I'd thought it was really worried me. I prayed, though still not really sure if God existed. I asked God if it was true that spiritualism was not of Him. I also asked if Jesus was indeed the Savior.

I wouldn't recommend doing this now, but I asked God what I should do about the spiritualist church. Then I opened the Bible randomly, closed my eyes, and stuck my finger on a scripture. It fell upon Jeremiah 7:4, "Do not trust in deceptive words and say, 'This is the temple of the Lord, the temple of the Lord, the temple of the Lord!'" The heading above the passage was "False Religion Worthless." It felt like God was saying to me, "Get out of spiritualism!"

It came as a great shock to think that spiritualism may not be of God, and I still wasn't convinced. I wondered if it was just a coincidence I'd found that verse.

The spirits attacked me that night. I slept with the lights on and the Bible on my bedside table. My husband was working the night shift at the hospital, and our son was staying over at my in-laws' home. So I was quite afraid to be alone with the spirits and my confused thoughts. It was a very restless night.

I was unaware that the Bible advises in 1 John 4:1–3, "Beloved, do not believe every spirit, but test the spirits, whether they are of God.... Every spirit that confesses that Jesus Christ has come in the flesh is of God, and every spirit that does not confess that Jesus Christ has come in the flesh is not of God. And this is the spirit of the Antichrist" (NKJV).

As I tried to sleep, the face of a particular Romany Gypsy kept popping into my mind, and I had such a desperate longing to see her. Once every year or two she would approach the homes in our neighborhood, offering to read our fortune. Some neighbors agreed to pay for hearing their future or for her lucky charms. I had a strong urge to see her and tell her the situation. But then I argued with myself that she wouldn't like hearing of the Pentecostal church and would only tell me to get back to the spiritualist church as soon as possible.

The very next morning the doorbell rang. Much to my delight, when I opened the door it was the Gypsy! She said she'd become a Christian recently and that the Lord had sent her to tell me. She also told me to throw out any charms she'd given me before. Other Gypsies she knew had also repented of the occult and found Jesus. They had been delivered of their psychic powers, and in time the Lord had begun to give them His gifts of the Holy Spirit instead. She chatted with me for a while and encouraged me to now accept Jesus into my heart as my personal Savior and Lord!

Part of me was drawn to Christ, but part of me was very wary. I wanted to be cautious. Afraid of being deceived again, I didn't want to jump in too suddenly. I was worried this might be just another religion that would also prove to be wrong and disappoint me or, worse still, cause me even more problems than before.

Was it true? Were spirits truly evil fallen angels? Had they existed for centuries possessing psychic knowledge of our families and historical figures down the generations? Was it true that they could easily disguise their evil form to pose as our deceased family or any famous celebrity who ever lived? Was Satan real or a myth? Were the spirits working through spiritualism actually evil and serving Satan in deceiving us? Or was spiritualism OK? Was it really of God after all?

It was a difficult and confusing time for me. I felt in a state of turmoil. So I decided to find out more before I reached a decision. If Jesus was the Savior, then I knew I would definitely want to accept Him. I was not fighting Him or being stubborn. I was fighting anxiety and confusion. I knew I was at a major crossroads, and it was serious, but I couldn't rush in.

During this time my Christian friend from the university and her church friends and pastor were all praying for me. Praise God! Over the next few days I read passages in the Bible warning against spiritualism. The following passage shocked me, "Do not let your people practice fortune-telling, or use sorcery, or interpret omens, or engage in witchcraft, or cast spells, or function as mediums or psychics, or call up spirits of the dead" (Deut. 18:10, NLT). I was stunned to read such things are an abomination to God.

Around this time I was also led to a verse that says, "And when they shall say unto you, Seek unto them that have familiar spirits, and unto wizard that peep, and that mutter: should not a people seek unto their God?" (Isa. 8:19, KJV). In the notes of the margin, the Bible took me by utter surprise. It explained that in Hebrew, the original Bible language, "familiar spirits" are translated as meaning demons or evil spirits. The Holy Spirit was opening my eyes and mind. Blessed be the precious name of the Lord! I suddenly realized that demons are psychic and thus very familiar with everything about our family history and us. It explained why demons impersonating the dead can tell us accurate things at séances!

It struck me that all the so-called spirit guides or guardian angels are actually very clever imposters, well able to impersonate the dead or pretend to be good angels of light with their centuries of knowledge about our ancestors. The Lord confirmed it with His precious Word: "For such men are false apostles.... And no wonder, for Satan himself masquerades as an angel of light. It is not surprising, then, if his servants masquerade as servants of righteousness" (2 Cor. 11:13–15).

I discovered the Bible shows in Hebrews 9:27 that when we die, we die *once* and face judgment. I realized there's no reincarnation or karma. Christians later explained the supernatural evidence that seems to prove reincarnation merely involves false visions granted by demons. And the Bible showed me there *is* a heaven and a hell. I learned Jesus is the only One who died for our sins and was resurrected.

Even religion encyclopedias listed no other religious leader or god who died for us or who shed his blood for our sin. "For there is one God and one mediator between God and men, the man Christ Jesus, who gave himself as a ransom for all" (1 Tim. 2:5–6). Spiritualist mediums are not the mediators between God and us; only Jesus Christ is.

The Lord was graciously opening my heart to truths in His Word that explained the false religion I had been in. The Scriptures showed me that spirits who work in spiritualism are thousands of years old, as they are fallen angels from Genesis times, and they are ruled by Satan. Isaiah 14:12 showed me why Lucifer fell from heaven. As demonic imposters, his minions wear masks and, being psychic, can mimic anyone who ever lived, pretending to be those individuals at séances. I was totally in awe of this revelation of the Lordship of Christ and the reality of the depth of deception He was rescuing me from.

The deception revealed through God's Word was a major key for me. Without it I probably would never have abandoned spiritualism completely and received Christ. It explained how all the mediums we knew, especially in the three different spiritualist churches, were also deceived by all the spirit guides. It explained why they couldn't adequately explain why our "good spirit guides" and relatives suddenly turned evil when we wanted *out* of spiritualism! This was crucial for my understanding. Spirits don't always harass psychics, New Agers. or spiritualists when they are doing their will; often they become nasty only when spiritualists attempt to sever ties with them.

If I had not known that the Bible shows demons are impersonators of the dead, I probably would have always continued to believe that Mum and I were just unlucky and had somehow attracted the wrong type of spirits to us. I'd have continued to believe we had mischievous or obnoxious spirits pretending to be my grandmother and sister, and that's why they later attacked us. It never before had crossed my mind as a spiritualist that *all* the spirits were imposters!

With this realization I could finally see that Jesus was God. The lovely Holy Spirit had patiently waited as the layers of falsehood were stripped away and the mental barriers broke down. I quickly renounced spiritualism and asked Jesus Christ into my heart. It was a very vulnerable time. I was delighted that I'd finally found the true God of love at last after all my years of searching for spiritual satisfaction within the New Age. However, there was a great deal of emotional and spiritual healing required. The Holy Spirit was to gently lead me on the road to restoration.

Deception Exposed

Realizing that you have been trusting and conversing with demons can leave you feeling unclean, disgusted, and horrified! When I realized how many years I had been deceived by spiritualism, I felt like spiritual rape had occurred. Also at my conversion there was a short period of bereavement. I felt a sense of sudden loss. I had to now properly grieve for my grandmother and sister, because I now realized that I couldn't talk with them like I'd thought I'd been doing for years.

There was anger to deal with too. Not at the mediums, as I loved them so dearly and knew they were also deceived. My anger was toward the demons for being so cruel and conning us all so completely. If you meet a New Ager or an ex-spiritualist who has just been born again, please be patient and sensitive with them. It's very likely they will be in a great deal of shock.

When I repented of the occult, I also asked Jesus to forgive me and cleanse me with His blood. It was an awesome thought to know He had become my Savior! When I received Him as my Lord, I had new hope and joy. There was less fear, worry, and so on. Plus, I felt God's overwhelming, tangible love. I had never felt His beautiful, breathtaking presence before.

At the advice of Christians, I gladly burned my many books, journals, and the like. They cautioned me to be thorough, to look at the backs of shelves and cupboards and find all books, recordings of spirit voices, and so on. In the first days of my conversion I devoured the Bible, reading all of the New Testament in less than a week. I read how witches in the Bible burned their occult paraphernalia at Ephesus when they converted (Acts 19).

I neglected university assignments that were due for submission to spend hours in the Bible instead. Jesus captivated me. He fascinated and delighted me. My university friend loaned me some of her worship CDs, and I played them repeatedly. I couldn't wait to go back to her church with her and attended every meeting I could.

I visited my mom in the hospital and shared what had happened to me. I felt a desperation to see her come to Christ and also be set free. Her first reaction was one of skepticism. She felt I had betrayed her and the movement. Even though her life was ruined by spiritualism, she still held an affinity for it and felt I was being a traitor by converting.

She eventually agreed to come to the Pentecostal church, saying she came only so she could have a few hours away from the hospital at the weekend. However, over time, the prayers of the church, the love and attention the Christians gave her, began to gradually break down her barriers.

Someone told me that Geordie Aitken, an ex-medium from Glasgow, would be speaking in a church near us. The person emphasized that there were not many ex-spiritualists who spoke in Christian gatherings. I knew it was an excellent opportunity for Mum to hear the truth about spiritualism, as she wasn't convinced when hearing it from me!

My friend took Mum and me along to hear Geordie testify. I was so disappointed that Mum seemed angry that night. She said Geordie was being unfair. She felt he was slamming spiritualism just because he had some bad experiences. She was still very sedated with the prescribed drugs and wasn't able to focus clearly on all he said.

Shortly after this I also heard of another ex-medium from Glasgow. Sadie Bryce had an audio recording of her testimony. I wrote to her. She phoned me and sent me a copy of her testimony. I prayed Mum would listen to it. I knew Mum would relate to her testimony, especially the part where Sadie explains that when she wanted to stop being a medium and get an ordinary career, all her spirit guides attacked her. (Audio of her testimony is available on YouTube.) Over the past fifteen years I have read in Christian magazines or saw on Christian TV other former mediums who had experienced this.

After sharing such testimonies with Mum, she agreed to come with a group from my church to see an evangelist at The Kelvin Hall in Glasgow. During the service she said she felt a sense of hope. Shortly after this night she too gave her heart to Jesus! She began to pray and seek the Lord, finding it difficult due to strong sedatives. Her heart's desire was to be released from the psychiatric hospital and for her flat to be free of demons. She came to church with me every Sunday and for midweek prayer meetings and Bible studies.

After months of heavy sedation Mum deliberately lied by telling the psychiatrists she no longer heard voices. She was hoping this would cause the hospital to discharge her. I didn't know of this until later. She could still hear the demons, but her faith was weak, and she chose to lie. She felt she couldn't fully trust Jesus to deliver her from the hospital. As her health had actually improved by now, the psychiatrist was convinced and discharged Mum from the hospital. I was so thrilled for her. Everyone at church joined in our rejoicing.

A Darker Tragedy

Sadly, Mum's flat was still demonized. When she returned home, she endured further harassment from spirits. My pastor was a new minister and had no experience with this kind of thing or with spiritually cleansing demonically possessed houses. Also, there was no deliverance ministry in that church then, although there is now. Back then, because Mum had just become a Christian, they didn't believe she could have any demon oppression or demonic problems.

Mum was still on heavy sedation. She'd urge me to warn everyone I knew about the truths of the occult and how it had affected her. We all kept praying for her, believing she would be healed. We had no idea she was still suffering from the same torment. I knew the demons were still in her flat, but she kept most of the torment from me as she didn't want me to be upset. She also didn't want to tell anyone about the spirits because she feared being readmitted to the psychiatric ward.

Mum and I stopped telling folks at church about the demons because we sensed they didn't believe us, thinking Mum was still mentally ill and imagining it all. In their minds we were both born again now, so we couldn't be having demonic problems. I even went to Mum's flat myself and tried to cast those demons out in Jesus's name, but I'd been saved only several months and did not yet know my authority in Christ or have a deliverance ministry yet.

One day an envelope arrived in my mother's handwriting. When I read her letter, I heard a very loud piercing scream, and then recognized it as my own. My mother wrote that she was about to commit suicide. I felt physically sick and yelled to my husband in sheer panic and horror. By the time my husband phoned an ambulance and the police, it was too late. Mum had obviously died the previous day, after mailing her letter.

I had always been very close to my mother. Maybe as an only child I was even closer to her than if I'd had siblings. I loved her very much and also admired her very kind and gentle manner, especially with animals. We shared so many interests. When she killed herself, I thought I could never, ever heal from the grief and shock. I kept trying to remind myself that demons couldn't torment her now, as she was safe in the loving, tender arms of Jesus.

However, in the first few weeks especially, I was plagued with images and thoughts of her final days, hours, and minutes. Such was my distress that my dear husband offered to take a week off from work to stay with me and look after me. I couldn't bear to be alone with my thoughts and so appreciated my husband's constant presence. For weeks I suffered from nightmares about Mum. Jesus was very close to me in those days. His presence comforted me, and I kept turning my thoughts to Him whenever I thought of Mum or had nightmares. During that time He did not leave me or forsake me. I felt like a wounded lamb He was carrying in His strong arms.

Losing my mother to an occult, demon-induced suicide was one of the greatest shocks in my life. The sadness of that incident cannot be adequately put into words. Satan may have thought he won a victory when my mom died, but he didn't! In the fifteen years since her death I have become even more determined to share my testimony. Perhaps if Mum hadn't taken her life, I wouldn't be quite as persistent in sharing. Every time I hear of someone being saved or helped when hearing my testimony, I believe Mum's death is not in vain.

Very soon after Mum's death, demons began to manifest in me. This can often happen in the early days of conversion for occultists who come to Christ. It may have been easy for occultists to throw out their occult paraphernalia and change their lifestyle, but it's not always easy to walk away from the effects it leaves. This should surely be another deterrent for anyone tempted to dabble in the occult!

I knew I needed the demons to be cast out in Jesus's name, but again, my pastor at that time couldn't accept that I needed deliverance. My pastor thought once you are saved, the demons *automatically* leave and thus don't need to be literally cast out. So when I manifested them, he assumed it wasn't demons but that I was just mentally ill or in shock over Mum's suicide. My worst nightmare nearly became my reality. After he saw me several times, and at the advice of others, my pastor told my husband to commit me to the nearest psychiatric hospital.

I couldn't believe it. Everyone, including the pastor, knew my mother had just been released from one and killed herself. Thankfully my husband knew it was a demonic problem and not a mental illness. I was so grateful to my husband for sparing me that nightmare. I knew as soon as psychiatrists saw demonic mani-festations through me, they'd diagnose me as mentally ill and hos-pitalize me immediately! I knew the psychiatrists would be very reluctant to ever release me from the hospital if the demons were not cast out. I'd been saved only a few months, yet I feared my fate would follow Mum's. I worried I would be tempted to commit sui-cide too. I thought how dreadful that would be for my dad, my hus-band, and our child.

Satan was no doubt angry that I'd left spiritualism and found Christ, but Jesus had the victory and would not allow Satan to destroy me. "The thief cometh not, but for to steal, and to kill, and to destroy: I am come that they might have life, and that they might have it more abundantly" (John 10:10, kjv). The Lord used my hus-band to preserve my life and not commit me to the psychiatric ward.

After some time of trusting Christ to end the demonic mani-festations while searching for a church, I found one that believed in deliverance and could help me. In that fellowship I learned the importance of daily obedience, sanctification, holiness, and death to self and the sinful nature. Also, they emphasized the centrality of developing an intimate, loving walk with Jesus. Worship was key. They often taught on abiding in Christ and entering into His presence.

One of their main aims was to help everyone fall deeper in love with Jesus and allow Him to bring them to new levels of glory in Him and maturity in their personal character. They ministered to me, and I was so grateful to God on the day my new pastor announced I was now free! Christ is faithful. He had gloriously set me free. Glory to His wonderful name!

My new pastor and assistant pastor had visited my mother's home and successfully cleansed it the first time they prayed. Spiritualists had kindly attempted before but not succeeded. When my pastor prayed, at the name of Jesus all the spirits left and never returned. About a year later I sold Mum's home without worrying the new tenants would be harassed.

Becoming a Witness

One day in church I asked the Lord what my calling was. I really hoped it was to become an evangelist to those in the occult. By now I was in my fourth and final year at university. The very next day after I prayed about my calling, I met five students or staff members at university who were psychics, spiritualists, or somehow dabbling in black magic.

Even when I had been in the occult I didn't meet five spiritualists in one year, never mind in one day! It seemed to confirm my heart's desire. Since then, over the past fifteen years, I've often met people, by apparent coincidences (God incidences), who tell me they are attending New Age or spiritualist meetings. By God's grace I share with them my testimony and about the true demonic identity of spirit guides.

When I was a New Age spiritualist, I never met any Christian who knew much about spiritualism or understood it from a biblical perspective. If someone had said he thought I was a devil worshipper and participated in sacrifices, I would have been really upset. I have heard of some who were accused of this, but spiritualists don't do those things. Once someone told me my faith was "of the devil," and though in retrospect I know that is very true, it didn't help me, because he didn't explain why he thought that way. If I had been shown relevant scriptures or testimonies, that would have spoken to me far more.

It's my heart's desire that Christians will be better equipped to explain what contemporary New Age spiritualists in Western cultures believe, and able to witness to them more effectively. Rather than saying to them, "Spiritualism is demonic," I humbly suggest we patiently dialogue with them first, listening and offering questions to help them contemplate the true and demonic source of their spiritual encounters and arrive at that conclusion themselves through the gentle prompting of the Holy Spirit.

Many people, even some Christians, feel that involvement in the

New Age is harmless. It may seem to be at just the mild side of the occult spectrum, but the demonic spirits behind spiritualism are the same spirits behind witchcraft and Satanism. The same spirits behind darker forms of the occult also empower the New Age and give psychic powers, "healing" abilities, and so on. New Age spiritualism is definitely *not* the same as Satanism, as some wrongly assume. However, they are at different ends of the same spiritual spectrum. The prominent New Age leader David Spangler even admits that in the New Age self-actualization process, "the being that helps man to reach this point is Lucifer."[3]

New Age beliefs are not new but are a mixture of ancient, pagan, or Eastern religions and mystical beliefs blended together. Their beliefs are full of complex, deep, and profound teachings that appear to fully support the logic behind their practices. Thus the New Age is persuasive and seems extremely credible. Many highly intelligent people and intellectuals adhere to the New Age movement.

Not that many years ago anyone with beliefs in the New Age or spiritualism would likely have been laughed at, but now it is acceptable and indeed commendable to hold such beliefs. There are varying levels of involvement in the New Age movement. Many individuals may participate lightly, perhaps as a form of entertainment, exercise, or relaxation, never considering themselves New Agers. Most of you will know a loved one or work colleague in this category. Other individuals will be more committed participants, regarding the New Age as their whole way of life.

Within the New Age there is always the potential for participants to graduate to deeper levels of involvement and even progress to darker forms of the occult. An interest in spiritualism is usually progressive too. Many spiritualists began with a little astrology then a little New Age, never anticipating they would develop an interest in spiritualism.

I'd like to emphasize that most New Agers and spiritualists are very ordinary people, usually very caring, kind-hearted, and lovable people on a search for spiritual truth. It is so sad that they are deceived into following this path. They aren't weird or evil as some people wrongly assume. That's a misconception.

If you told them you thought their beliefs or practices were evil, they would be horrified, as they believe spiritualism to be good and wholesome. They most certainly would be very upset if you suggested they were a sorcerer or Satanist! Most New Agers and spiritualists disagree with black and even "white" magic.

New Age followers welcome the Dawn of the New Age, or Age of Aquarius, during the Last Days. During this end time in history they feel humanity is entering a Golden Age, where more cultures (including more Western societies) will reject their traditional faiths to come together in the New Age movement, accepting their belief that all paths lead to God. Indeed, the New Age movement continues to see massive growth globally today. And they believe even more people will accept New Age beliefs, psychic phenomena, and so on, and that such a one-world religion or movement will usher in peace.

Many New Age adherents believe in the Last Days, a Messiah-like figure will appear to bring global peace. Rather than the biblical Jesus, they believe this man to be an ascended master, or spiritual being who has lived through many reincarnations. They feel that this New Age christ-spirit will be a redeemer for all religions: the Krishna for Hindus, the Messiah for Jews, the Maitreya for Buddhists, the Virgin Mary for Catholics, and so on. This highlights their belief that all religions lead to God and that they don't accept Christ as the only Savior or the only way to the heavenly Father.

There is a wide range of practices within the New Age movement, and participants will largely pick and choose which activities they like, whether reiki, yoga, crystal healing, meditation, past life regression, tarot cards, and so on. Most of them will visit tarot card parties, psychic fairs, New Age bookstores, etc. They will usually be keen to use alternative health remedies, alternative therapies, relaxation techniques, and listen to New Age music, among other things. Often there will be new fads that become popular and offer the New Ager a new level of spiritual growth or enlightenment, or a new and very *real* mystical experience.

Angel craze has increased in recent years. New Age self-proclaimed "angel experts" encourage people to buy angelic merchandise and pray to angelic beings, often convincing them that they are God's holy angels or archangels such as the biblical Michael or Gabriel. Some "angel experts" also encourage people to call on Uriel, Raphael, and other angels from the apocryphal First Book of Enoch, a nonbiblical text. Angel experts claiming to receive information from such guardian angels are actually channeling teachings and doctrines of devils. The Bible tells us, "In later times some will abandon the faith and follow deceiving spirits and things taught by demons" (1 Tim. 4:1).

Many New Age activities are being practiced by the ordinary everyday person, who may not even be actually interested in New Age. Yet they receive its influence unawares. Relaxation techniques and even some physical therapies contain New Age exercises. Acupuncture, reflexology, and visualization techniques involve spiritual "energies," whether or not the therapist or clients realize that. Health centers offer their patients reiki, a relaxation technique that originated in Japan, yet many are unaware that it involves the transmission of healing from reiki spirit guides.

The top founders and leaders of the New Age movement, such as the late mediums Madame Blavatsky and Alice Bailey, as well as current-day leaders such as mediums Benjamin Creme and David Spangler, welcomed and promoted the New Age movement's recent shift toward influencing society and mainstream culture. Such leaders have freely admitted they adhere to a Luciferian Doctrine![4]

Within yoga even the trained yogis admit the basics of the first stage in yoga are designed to attain mystical union with the Universal Spirit. Yogis warn that yoga, transcendental meditation, and opening the *chakras* can arouse dangerous supernatural forces, especially the *kundalini* (which means "coiled one") serpent spirit of the spinal base *chakra*.

Yogis also admit that the main aim for practicing yoga is not merely to relax or enjoy gentle exercise but to gain occult powers. Whether those who participate in basic yoga for relaxation are or are not interested in its spirituality, they have literally opened doors to spiritual entities. Christian minister Mike Shreve, a former top yoga tutor, explains this on his website, www.thetruelight.net.

SPIRITUALISM: BELIEFS AND PRACTICES

The majority of spiritualists also adhere to most beliefs of the New Age movement, such as reincarnation, and participate in many New Age activities, such as meditation, but they do not necessarily follow all New Age practices.

There are a few different strands of spiritualism. For example, some cultures will practice spiritualism mixed with animism, shamanism, or witchcraft—a very dangerous concoction. Even some Satanists use spiritualism. But the most common type and the one we are most likely to encounter is the contemporary New Age spiritualism of Western cultures, where practitioners will describe themselves as spiritualists or "light workers." This *seems* milder than other forms of occultism and is far more accepted in mainstream societies today.

All spiritualists believe they can communicate with dead relatives. Most mediums are caring and have kind motives; they genuinely desire to comfort the bereaved in this way. They are hungry for spiritual truths and growth, and sadly can't see that Satan has tricked them.

They believe they can also communicate with wise spiritual beings who offer people counsel, healing, or hidden knowledge of the future. The promise of secrets revealed by occult methods fascinates and draws many recruits. These entities can also administer and train the spiritualist in supernatural or psychic abilities.

Mediums classify these entities as being spirit or healing guides, guardian angels, or ascended masters. Rather than trusting the Holy Spirit for direction, they trust in those spirits.

All of the gifts we see operating in the Bible and in some Christian churches today have a demonic counterpart in spiritualist churches. Satan gives spiritualists, psychics, and some New Agers supernatural abilities. These abilities are empowered by Satan's servants, the demonic spirits, and thus are actually counterfeit copies of the gifts of the precious Holy Spirit of God.

Sadly, spiritualists are not aware of this true source of their powers or of the true identity of the masquerading demons that can impersonate the dead. Thus, where Christian churches see healings, miracles, dreams, and visions, so do spiritualist churches. Where Christians may speak prophecies or words of knowledge under the inspiration of the Holy Spirit, spiritualists do the same but under demonic influence. Where Christians teach from the Bible, spiritualists do also but not exclusively. They will also teach from a variety of religious traditions or New Age philosophies.

Similarly, astral projection, or soul travel, is the demonic counterfeit of the Holy Spirit–empowered disappearance and reappearance of Phillip after he baptized the Ethiopian eunuch, (Acts 8:39). Psychics' claims to have experienced astral projection among the planets is similar to the biblical experience of the man of God who was "caught up to the third heaven" (2 Cor. 12:2).

While Christians pray to see the Lord heal the sick, spiritualists see "healings" too. Where Christians raise the dead, spiritualists believe they do that too. They believe they have raised the dead temporarily while channeling and conversing with an apparent dead relative at a séance. Where Christians speak in other tongues, the tongues of men and of angels, spiritualists feel they do likewise when allowing their dead relatives or spirit guides to speak "through" them.

There are many warnings about spiritualism, false angels, false Christs, and demonic-inspired doctrines in the Bible, and about their increase in the last days. But spiritualists and light workers believe the Bible was altered. They feel such warnings were added later to deliberately discount spiritualism.

As the English vicar Kevin Logan wrote in the book *Paganism and the Occult*, spiritualists "overlook Jesus' specific illustration of the barrier which prevents real contact between the spirit-world and earth."[5] The Bible highlights that communication with the dead is impossible (Luke 16:26). Once dead, we cannot return to earth. After judgment we enter heaven or hell and can't return to talk to the living. Unknown to spiritualists, demons take advantage of the human desire to communicate with the deceased and impersonate their dead loved ones.

Spiritualists certainly don't believe these realities, however. They don't accept the Bible as the infallible Word of God. Some believe Jesus maybe was the Son of God, but that He was more likely a great psychic healer, spiritualist medium, or ascended master. They don't believe in the biblical heaven or hell. They don't believe anyone goes to hell after death, but rather to one of many planes depending on our works. Then there's the opportunity to reincarnate into a new person on earth, do more good deeds to balance out our karma in that life, and thus reach a higher plane next time we die. Spiritualism thus doesn't see the need of a Savior, forgiveness, or salvation. They don't believe we need Christ's blood to cleanse us.

Spiritualists will ignore the Bible's warnings on attempting to communicate with the dead. They feel such warnings are merely scare tactics from domineering Christians who are fearful of the practice. Indeed, spiritualists feel the prophecies, healings, and miracles throughout the Bible are actually examples of psychic powers and were not empowered by the Holy Spirit at all.

To reiterate, if you told a spiritualist that you thought their beliefs or practices were evil, or that Satan was the source of their spiritual abilities, they would be horrified and assume you were cruel or rude to suggest such a thing. They genuinely believe it all to be good, wholesome, and helpful, especially for grieving families. They sincerely feel they are doing God's will.

At spiritualist churches, in halls, or in homes, those gathered will typically have a churchlike meeting. This involves hymns and a short address on topics concerning good morality, or the enduring love and guidance our departed family members still have for us. Then there follows a demonstration of spiritualism itself, whereby the platform medium will attempt to communicate with the dead. She will see and hear spirits of so-called dead relatives giving "messages" from them to the audience. Many in the audience won't be able to see or hear the spirits, unless they are psychic or training in mediumship too.

There are set days for psychic healing, where the medium will lay hands on the patient and transmit healing energies from their "spirit guide" to heal that individual. Mediums are also involved in rescue work, where they apparently help the deceased or "trapped souls" move to higher realms.

You may have heard of the movie *The Haunting in Connecticut*. Some of the activities depicted in the film truly do occur! My mother attended transfiguration sessions, and she took me with her on one occasion. During this phenomenon the spirits are evident not only to the medium but also to the whole congregation. The medium must go into a deep trance to enter another state of consciousness and allow the spirits to come through her body. The medium's face will appear to change, and the face of the dead relative will appear instead, as if his features are superimposed onto the medium's features.

When the entity speaks, family members will easily recognize it as the voice of their deceased loved one. The spirit will then give accurate information to convince the family it truly is him and that he has been lovingly watching the daily activities of their lives since his death. This comforts many, especially the recently bereaved. If it's a spirit guide who materializes, he will most likely claim to be a Red Indian chief, and that he has been sent to advise the client and guide him through his life. He may advise the person on what career to pursue or which person to marry, and so on.

The advanced transfiguration sessions are even more convincing. A misty substance they call ectoplasm, which resembles hanging icicles, protrudes from the trance medium's mouth and nose. It solidifies into a "dead spirit" or "dead relative." It then walks and talks, still attached to the medium by a thin strip. Then it gives personal messages to the congregation.

Even mediums admit this is a dangerous practice. If touched by a spectator without the medium's previous permission, the spirit can retract suddenly, reentering the medium's body before turning back into fluid ectoplasm. When these spirits retract in their solid form, it can cause mediums to collapse, become crippled, or even die.

Raphael Gasson, a famous former medium from England, knew of mediums temporarily blinded in this way. He wrote of it in his 1972 book, *The Challenging Counterfeit*. Another former medium from the United States, Victor Ernest, knew of mediums who were either admitted to psychiatric hospitals because they attempted to take their own lives or were visited by Satan, who tried to induce them to commit suicide. Ernest wrote of such accounts in his 1970 book, *I Talked With Spirits*.

Some Christians think such phenomena are impossible and either merely figments of imagination or the work of frauds, but it's very tangible and real. Ectoplasm is the name given to the substance that exudes from the medium's body and combines with the spirit entity. When I was younger, I watched my mother and others touch the ectoplasm that had come out of the medium's mouth. They told me it was a real substance and felt like thin moist muslin or a spider's web. I saw it but didn't want to touch it!

Ben Alexander, a former medium from England, wrote of the reality of transfigurations in his 2005 book *Out From Darkness*. Even scientists found hard evidence when submitting such activity to their scientific tests. During a séance, when the medium went into deep trance, everyone in the room felt the temperature drop. When ectoplasm exuded from the medium, the scientists weighed her, comparing the result with her pre-trance weight of minutes before. She had lost 54.5 pounds of weight, recovering it when the trance ended and the ectoplasm returned to her body. As Alexander stated, "This fact is another proof of Satan extracting the life force out of a person for his own needs."[6]

Some practices used in spiritualism and the New Age movement, such as transcendental meditation, yoga, hypnosis, and reiki have seen massive growth in mainstream society. Shunned for decades, they have infiltrated the culture and become very acceptable in the health care, counseling, and psychology fields; among self-improvement specialists; in relaxation therapies; and even in some churches. Most people embrace these practices without knowing the true demonic source behind them or the potential dangers involved.

A FINAL WORD

I hope I've provided some insight into what spiritualists and light workers believe and practice in contemporary Western cultures. I've tried to show their motives are kind and genuine, albeit deceived.

I'd like to emphasize it's not my intent to stimulate hysteria or fascination with spiritualism, but we can't sit on the fence either. Spiritualism is a tool of Satan and an enemy of Christianity. They are as different as black and white. Spirits aim to lead people away from believing in Christ, enticing them with occult diversions, and fostering dependence on spirit guides and psychic powers instead of the Bible and Holy Spirit for direction and power.

Occult involvement is usually progressive, starting with milder forms in the New Age, but often leading a person to develop psychic powers and to progress to spiritualism, Wicca, or the like. Years ago it was mostly only spiritualists, witches, Satanists, and those in Eastern religions who practiced yoga, transcendental meditation, acupuncture, holistic medicine, martial arts, reiki, and so on. But now we see these practices everywhere. These activities may seem mild, even harmless, but they are still within the same demonic range, empowered by Satan's counterfeit sources.

After reading my chapter, please don't dwell on spiritualism. I don't desire to glorify the darkness, but only to exalt the name of Jesus Christ alone. As you and I know, salvation is only in Christ, and only He has all the answers people search for in the New Age.

Also, please don't be afraid to witness to New Agers. You don't have to fear demonic beings—"You, dear children, are from God and have overcome them, because the one who is in you is greater than the one who is in the world" (1 John 4:4).

RECOMMENDED RESOURCES

For further resources on reaching New Age spiritualists, I recommend the following websites, which can refer visitors to ministries that help those who have been involved in spiritualism:

- Reach Out Trust, www.ReachOutTrust.org

- Spotlight Ministries, www.SpotlightMinistries.org.uk

- Spiritual Counterfeits Project, www.scp-inc.org

Laura Maxwell grew up near Glasgow, Scotland. She graduated from Strathclyde University with an honors degree in psychology and was involved in teaching art to disabled adults. She is a member of The Scottish Fellowship of Christian Writers. Her articles and poetry have been featured in magazines and broadcast on radio in Europe and beyond. She also has shared her testimony in churches, Christian conferences, and on satellite TV and radio stations across Europe. She lives with her family.

Chapter 7

ESCAPING THE VAMPIRE'S LAIR

By Brian Reed

W HEN JEFF HARSHBARGER first approached me about contributing to this book, I was reluctant to share what I've been through, given the stupidity of my choices. The consequences of my actions will follow me for the rest of my life. Anyone who finds out what I've been involved in either shuns me or lifts me onto some kind of pedestal as if I'm some kind of expert on all things occult. Both reactions are hard to grapple with. Nonetheless, believing I could be a vampire is the worst decision I have ever made, and I hope my story can help someone else.

My life started out innocently enough. I was brought up in a small town and attended a middle-of-the-road kind of church. Not liberal, not conservative, just a bunch of middle-class people paying homage every Sunday to a God who, to me at least, seemed far away. There was kind of a natural separation in this congregation. The adults all sat together on the main floor of the church while kids went to children's church in an entirely different area. Meanwhile anyone old enough for youth group sat in the balcony, mostly to make fun of the bell choir or the pastor or, if you sat in just the right place, to catch a nap without being noticed.

I was skinny, not exactly athletic, and usually the brunt of jokes. I never felt like I fit in, especially in this church. But I attended because I wanted to be a good person and because my parents attended and because up in the corner of that balcony I would have an entire hour of uninterrupted reading. To say I was a bookworm is an understatement. I read everything from a particular series about a boy wizard to comic books to anything else I could get my hands on. I loved the way an hour in a good book could take me completely away from the boring, humiliating life I led.

On the other side of the coin, being a voracious reader seemed to put me in a class all by myself. People would tell me I was smart, and I believed them. Reading made my parents proud—so proud they never made an issue of the fact that I read during church. They actually encouraged me. Never once did they check to see exactly what I read. Even though my ego soon became inflated, I still felt like such an outsider and held my classmates in contempt.

Any child without guidance is in for trouble. When that child reaches high school and still has no real parameters, life can become hellish. I was quiet and seemed compliant because I didn't say much. I didn't say much because the adults in the books I read never seemed to understand people my age, so I reasoned neither would the adults around me. Inside I began to feel quite a bit of angst toward almost everyone around me. I began to dream about beating people up and committing suicide. But, like I said, because my façade was good, I was left to my own devices.

In my junior year of high school I had put aside the books about boy wizards and the children of Olympian gods, considering them youth well spent, and began to scan the shelves of my local bookstore for deeper things. I no longer wanted to read about people who lived fantastic lives; I longed to experience the fantastic myself.

I liked the idea of being able to say I attended church, but I figured it would always be there. At this point in my life church didn't actually satisfy my spiritual curiosity. It felt so milquetoast and hollow, and I wanted to expand my mind. So I began my quest.

I remember looking through the sci-fi section of the bookstore. I'd read most of what I saw, so I perused the fantasy books, my personal favorite. How often I wished I could step through a door and become a hero with a sword. Then I rounded the corner. I beheld an entire shelving system labeled "New Age." Spiritism was something

I really didn't know much about, or did I? There were those two Wiccan girls in my humanities class. Weren't they all about nature? And wasn't there a kids' show about a psychic girl? And what about that boy wizard I had grown up reading about? I'd always wanted magick to be real. What if it could be?

I scanned the shelves. Books on witchcraft and palmistry caught my eye. I pictured myself, kind of Houdini style, leading people in a séance. There was a book on tarot cards and a satanic bible. No touching that. I'd read enough to know what happened to bad wizards. Then I saw something really interesting: a book that told the history of the vampire. I had read some woman's story about a vampire's life just last month and loved it. This I could sink my teeth into, so to speak.

I bought my book. I spent way too much money on the thing, but I didn't care. It was beautifully bound in cloth with many stories, illustrations, and what appeared to be actual photographs. I couldn't wait to get it home. I read through dinner and on into the evening. Sometime around 2:00 a.m. I lifted my weary eyes from the pages. The house seemed extra quiet. My parents said good night hours ago. But still, somehow, I felt as though I was not alone.

I figured I must have spooked myself with stories of things that appear out of nowhere to suck blood. Maybe I'd read enough for one evening. I closed the book and went to my computer. I pulled up a search engine and typed "vampire." So many websites came up I couldn't count them all. Some gave the very stories I had just read; some told of real encounters.

I read about a group that actually claimed to be a church for vampires where everyone dressed like Bela Lugosi. That would be fun. Then I read about a particular kind of vampires who called themselves psychic. They didn't play by the same rules. They didn't burn at sunrise, they didn't need an invitation to come into my house, and the Christian cross didn't frighten them. When in their meditative state, these psychic vampires could go anywhere through something called astral projection. Their goal was not to suck actual blood but rather a person's "life force." Life force equaled power. How intriguing.

I read the web page again. These people said they were set apart, that they were a breed above normal man. Wasn't that me? Wasn't I the smartest, the most cunning? Hadn't I hid my true nature from everyone, including my parents? I leaned back in my chair and imagined what it would be like to live a new life of power, how good it would feel to get back at all the people who'd picked on me.

Then I felt it again, the overwhelming silence, and in that silence, the presence. I didn't know what else to call it. I felt as though it peered over my shoulder at the computer screen I viewed. Maybe it was a psychic vampire, I teased myself. I turned quickly and saw no one, but the feeling did not go away. I closed my laptop, not bothering to actually shut it down, and crawled into bed to try to sleep.

My journey had begun. I lived each day with a new fervor. I was normal by day so no one suspected my covert life. I studied hard and earned good grades. I was proud of my intellectual abilities and certain that my higher intelligence indicated the latent vampire inside. As long as my grades were good and my manner pleasing, my parents let me do whatever I wanted.

At night, after everyone in the house went to sleep, I scoured the Internet. I studied everything I could put my hands on. Some vampires were Satanists; some were into witchcraft. Some simply enjoyed life as a vampire without the religious trappings. Most at one point or another drank blood. Not much, I learned. Human blood represented our true life force, but drinking too much could make a person sick.

So, it seemed, the psychic vampire, was the direction that called to me. I needed to learn how to take a person's life force. In order to do that, I needed a mentor. I needed to discuss what I was learning.

BECOMING A VAMPIRE

The computer screen flickered. There were all kinds of ways I could connect. Social media became my church. Through it I met others like me. I soon learned how to meditate. Through meditation I met the presence that now constantly hung around me. She called herself Oshi, a vampire who lived in ancient Egypt. I had a mentor and a guide.

Oshi first taught me how to take the life force from someone in the same room as me. I began by practicing on my annoying younger brother. When he became whiny, I would concentrate and see, in my mind at least, his energy seeping out his feet and then into mine. Eventually he would quiet down and take a nap.

What had I done? I felt like a murderer. I believed I had taken life from my own brother, and the sick part of it was that I felt energized, more alive than ever. Did this really happen? Looking back, I don't think so. A kid who stays up past his bedtime is liable to be cranky and eventually fall asleep. But at the time I firmly believed I wanted to be powerful so badly. That day I knew I had stepped over the threshold. I had awakened a thirst for something, and now I only wanted more.

So I tried it at school on teachers and people I didn't like, which by now was most everyone. I no longer cared about being popular; I remained quiet. I thought it very funny that no one knew what hid beneath my mask. I also found some friends; at least I thought they were friends. Some people called us geeks, some intellectuals. We spent hours together discussing various aspects of the occult, listening to thrash metal, and entertaining ourselves with role-playing games. We all took different aspects of power. One friend was a druid, one the wizard, one the ranger (a warrior who walks alone). I, of course, was the vampire.

At night I continued to spend time with Oshi. I thought I was good at taking energy, so I decided to try my hand at astral projection. The first time I did it I felt like I had floated to a corner of my room on the ceiling. Then suddenly I fell into my body. The sensation of falling so frightened me I refused to try again for several nights. However, with Oshi's help, in time I began to travel almost nightly.

Three years later I was in college. I was an intellectual, and I was an occultist. When people asked me what I was, as people are inclined to do, occultist is what I told them. The vampire in me only emerged around people of my own kind.

On the inside, however, I was tormented. No one knew just what a monster I was. It was about this time that I began to hear Oshi everywhere I went. I knew eventually I would kill myself, and we would spend eternity together.

But life went on. I studied philosophy and English literature. I showed up at my parents' church at the holidays. After all, everyone thought I was a good person, and a vampire is never known for what he really is. Besides, I had read that Christian holidays stemmed from pagan ones. Why not celebrate?

The more vampire stuff I read, the more vampirelike I became, but probably not in the way you're thinking. Hollywood loves to glamorize the covert seduction associated with the traditional vampire. The idea of an innocent victim becoming eternally damned along with him seems to appeal to a lot of people.

However, what comes across the silver screen is cartoonlike compared to the real thing. There are no Transylvanian accents or black capes, no covens of us living in New Orleans, and thank goodness no one sparkles in the sunlight. The only similarity with Hollywood's depiction is that a vampire wants to blend in with society and not be noticed. I actually looked more like a condescending preppie.

Soon I thought I was an expert on meditation and astral projection. I believed Oshi was my best friend, and I was convinced that I loved her. I thought I could go anywhere, and I did almost every night. The scary part was when I traveled without wanting to because I felt I needed energy to live the next day. When that happened, instead of feeling energized I would wake up worn out and exhausted.

But still I pursued more targets. I would scout my victims through the week. Usually I would choose people I felt deserved to be sucked of life: a professor who had wronged someone, for example, or an athlete who demanded worship. When a particular person caught my eye, I would follow him and get what I thought was a feel for his life force. At night I would take a journey to the home of my victim and concentrate on stealing his or her life's energy.

Perhaps because of my interest in vampirism, I found it easier to make friends in college. I met so many more people who shared my interests. All of my friends dabbled in some form of occult, and all had the same love of the vampire that I did. We rented a house just off campus, which we dubbed our lair. We hung crystals and dream catchers and pictures of dragons and knights and trolls all around the place.

One of the women who lived with us stands out in my memory. I'll call her Guinevere, though she actually went by an elaborate, gothic name we were happy to call her. I liked Guinevere. A lot. She became the bright spot in my horrible existence. Maybe because she reminded me of my spirit guide. Or maybe because she practiced what I thought was a cool form of witchcraft. The left hand path, she called it.

I told her about Oshi, and in a meditative state she used to channel her for me. We spent about a year together. It was with Guinevere that I first drank human blood. I won't go into detail except to say, once again, that human beings *cannot* drink human blood without becoming very sick.

The day I first drank blood is etched in my memory as the day things in my wretched existence started to go horribly wrong. I remember being relatively high at a party and performing a kind of ceremony with my friends. Several people had slit their hands and let their blood drip into a cup. The cup was passed around. Of course, thinking I was superior, I took more than just a sip of the blood. Then I chased it with beer.

The physical reaction was almost immediate, and I found myself upchucking the disgusting cocktail. Everyone around me laughed and pointed as I hung my head over a very dirty commode. My debasement was very funny to them, but it infuriated me. Later that night Guinevere said my problem was that I had no connection to the blood of the people from the party. But if she and I exchanged blood, we would be forever bound body and spirit. So we exchanged each other's blood. Often.

Once we were bound eternally, our relationship changed. Guinevere and I started to fight. She wanted to control me, and I wanted to control her. After a while, being the entirely selfish creatures we were, my eternal soul mate and I went our separate ways.

I fled right into the arms of my spirit guide, but for the first time instead of acceptance I felt anger. I knew without a doubt that if I didn't do as she told me, she would kill me.

Now it might sound funny to the average person that an occultist, a vampire who had dealt with this kind of thing for years, would be afraid, but I was. I was petrified that Oshi would attack me, that I would wake to find her in my room and not be able to control her. Or, my worst nightmare, that Oshi would take me on an astral travel to the clouds and just let me fall. I felt that if I ever hit the ground in one of those sessions, I would wake up dead.

So I finally lived a vampire's life; I sank into depression. I pulled away from everyone and everything. I stopped going to class. I spent most of my days alone, cutting myself to taste my own blood. I would sleep through the day and stay awake all night. I lost my appetite for food, except for sweets. I survived on Mountain Dew and beer.

I remember one evening walking through my apartment. At this point I lived alone. I went into the bathroom without turning the light on because light hurt my eyes. I looked at my image in the mirror and finally saw what I thought I always I wanted. A man looked back at me—pale, emaciated, deep circles under his eyes, hair a mess. I looked like death. I looked like a vampire.

Then, in the mirror, a shadow on the wall became clearer. It was Oshi; I knew it was. And I knew she was no guide. I could never actually see her, though I thought I could. What I knew for sure was that the sense of anger and evil in the bathroom was palatable, and it frightened me so I could barely move. In that moment I knew Oshi was evil and dangerous, that she didn't love me but wanted nothing more than to kill me. And I knew I'd had enough.

I moved to a new apartment and got rid of all my vampire/occult stuff. I wanted to be normal, and I felt if I changed my environment, I would change too. I changed my major and went back to class. But I still heard my guide at times during the day even though I made every effort to shut her out. She taunted me, whispering, "You need that person. You can't avoid what you are. You need energy. You can't live without me." I wondered if I might be schizophrenic. At night instead of traveling, I suffered horrible nightmares of being trapped in a house unable to escape and sometimes of being dragged below the earth.

About that time two things happened at once. I met another girl, an English major who seemed different from the people I hung with. She laughed easily and listened when I spoke. I'll call her Laurie. She wasn't put off when I told her what I had been involved in. I noticed she had a Bible among her books, so I told her I used to go to church. She invited me to her Bible study.

The other thing that happened was that I developed a cold that would not go away.

I'll never forget the first time I went to Laurie's Bible study. It was off campus in a small house. I walked in feeling awkward, and I couldn't figure out why. I still visited my parents' church when I went home on occasion. And I still firmly believed that Christians were simply pagans at the roots of their religion. I determined to fit in.

But these people bothered me. They seemed more alive. More

real. And when they looked at me, I wanted to look away. *But why?* These people didn't know what I had done. They didn't know that I felt like such a failure. I figured the power I had worked so hard to achieve had driven me to insanity. I didn't know what made me so nervous. But for some reason when they started to sing, I wanted to run out the door.

A man got up from the group. There was nothing special about him. Wearing blue jeans and a T-shirt, he began to talk about Jesus. The man spoke as if Jesus were a close friend. He talked about love and told his own story. He told a story of a guy named Paul and a woman who was a psychic. He said Paul prayed for her to be freed from the demon. My heart went cold. I could feel Oshi. I could feel her anger.

Then I got angry. That couldn't be me. I could never be like that psychic woman. She was completely possessed and owned by a spirit; I thought I was still in control. But the image of the shadow in the bathroom had been burned into my memory. Just thinking about it made me shudder. I realized that I might not be able to control Oshi. This realization combined with the nightmares I'd been having made me angry, because I did not want to see the truth.

I decided that this man must be my enemy. Even though I had sworn to give it up, I would travel once again. He would be my next victim.

That night I lay in bed, trying to concentrate as I used to and travel to the man's home to take his life force. But instead of being transported to another place, nothing happened. I tried again. I closed my eyes and tried to feel light. Just as quickly, my eyes popped open and I lay alone in my room. Where had Oshi gone? I couldn't feel her anywhere. I thought about the man I was trying to attack—just a normal thirty-something guy with a smile like John Denver's. I felt a wave of remorse. He was a good man. But I determined to try again.

I closed my eyes and tried to concentrate. Nothing at all. But then I noticed a new presence, one I had never felt before. I opened my eyes and knew God was in the room.

How did I know? His presence was like nothing I had ever encountered. It frightened me to the core but not because it felt evil. Evil will make you afraid. I was frightened because this presence was good, and I knew I was evil. This being had every right to condemn me, and there was no question that He could.

I rolled out of bed and onto my knees. Remembering some of what I'd learned in church all those years, I asked Jesus to come into my life that night. I never heard from Oshi again.

Years later I still follow Him. Is my life perfect? Not at all. I battle depression, I'm still skinny, and I now have HIV either from my past drug use or from exchanging contaminated blood. The lingering cold I had developed was the first sign. But when I think back to all I've come from—the loneliness, the suicidal thoughts, and never feeling accepted—I now can see God's hand on my life. I was rebellious. I was proud. And when I realize that God took the time to save me, my heart rejoices. Whom the Son sets free is free indeed.

LIGHT IN THE DARKNESS

It is understandable that many Christians would be unsure how to help someone who is involved in the occult. But if my story does anything, I pray that it will help someone escape the misery I experienced as a result of my participation in vampirism. I believe the church can help those drifting toward the occult as well as those longing to escape its grasp. If you will indulge me, I would like to share some of my thoughts on how you can reach out to others who may be drifting toward the same dangerous path I once found myself on.

When I did attend church as a kid, I felt invisible. Daily, in thousands of churches across America, there are countless kids who feel that way too. I can't count how often I heard it said from the pulpit that the youth are the church of the future or that they are the church of tomorrow. Now, I know the good intentions of those who spoke those words. However, back then, what I heard and what I felt was that we, the youth, were not the church right now. Youth and children need to feel included not separated.

The younger generation needs to be reached. So I'm asking you, the reader, to build a bridge with at least one child, teen, or young adult. Their lives may depend on it. One day they may simply walk out of the church and never return because they didn't feel loved, were never included, or were pushed over into a program that separated them from the rest of the body.

Speaking of youth programs, I noticed when I was growing up that the people who worked with children or youth didn't stay at the church very long. These were the people us kids could build a relationship with, and all too frequently they would come and go with no explanation. Having someone who can see an entire class of kids through high school will make a profound impact on their lives. Those four or five years will give the youth time to develop a lasting relationship with a trusted mentor who can help guide them during those crucial years.

The other part of my story is that though I grew up in a church, I was not encouraged to have a relationship with Jesus. People saw the books I read, and no one said I shouldn't read them or even suggested a good alternative. Reading for the sake of reading is not always a good thing.

Please get rid of the mind-set that a book or movie published for kids is healthy for kids. Next time you're in a bookstore, look through the children's section. Then move to the section for young adults. From the cradle all the way through college, popular books are laced with magick and occult themes. It's hard to find anything published of late that is truly wholesome. Pay attention to the sites your children visit on the Internet. I was able to find a lot of support for my occult leanings online.

The key to helping other young people avoid the trap I fell into is simple. It's time. Invest time with a child or young person in your church who might need your influence, and you will make a difference.

Brian Reed is a schoolteacher in a small town in the Northwest. He still enjoys reading and spending time with his wife and three children.

Chapter 8

FREED FROM SATAN'S GRASP

By Vince McCann

I F YOU HAVE never dabbled in the occult, it may be difficult to understand how a person could be drawn into its beliefs and practices. I hope that my story will help Christians see why people choose to be involved in the occult, how we can approach them, and what our attitude should be toward them.

Twenty years ago I was a teenager, and like many other young people I felt something was missing in my life. So I embarked upon a journey that led to me into the Goth and punk scene and into alcohol and drug abuse. The music, the Goth image, and the drinking and drugs never really satisfied me, so I turned my attention to the spiritual realm. It seemed most natural to turn to the church, but I quickly dismissed that thought because of the few churches I had attended. The buildings were dark, cold, and uninviting, and the services were much too long. It was a chore to sit through the entire service. I recall people mumbling the hymns halfheartedly, glancing at their watches, and gazing around as if their minds were elsewhere. God seemed distant and elusive in these places.

Not finding God in the churches I had been exposed to, I turned my attention to the occult. It seemed to provide the answers I was looking for and felt comfortable to me. And it was exciting. The occult also gave me the sense that I was discovering esoteric knowledge, that I was one of only a few to learn these secrets, which appealed to my pride.

Because I was not finding the spiritual satisfaction that only God can provide through a relationship with Christ, I kept feeling compelled to go deeper and deeper into different aspects of the occult. This led to me calling directly on demonic spirits and eventually becoming involved with a girl who was totally controlled by demons. Months of extreme and frightening supernatural torment, deception, and evil followed, and it nearly was the end of me. But a miraculous chain of events occurred, and God came to my aid in a dramatic way. (I share my complete testimony in my book, *Freed From Satan's Grasp*.)

It is tragic to think that if I hadn't been exposed to the dry and lifeless versions of Christianity in my earlier years, I may not have experimented with dark alternative spirituality and could have been spared the hell I endured. The experiences I had with some of those churches are enough to turn not only young people away from Christianity but also just about anyone.

Especially worrying is the fact that God seemed uninvolved in the lives of those attending the churches I visited in my youth. Such churches, however, are not a true reflection of what Christianity should be. Christianity, as God intended it to be, is vibrant and life affirming, a place where God is intimately involved and active in the life of the congregation as a whole as well as the individual. Thankfully, there are also many churches around where Christ's love is found at work through the people. These churches are alive and move in God's supernatural power.

I believe this latter point is especially important in our current, occult-saturated society. People are not only physical beings but also spiritual beings. As such, every person, whether he recognizes it or not, has spiritual needs that must be met. The mathematician and philosopher Blaise Pascal said that every person has a God-shaped void within him. If someone fails to experience the supernatural work of God in a church, he is going to look for another means to fill that void. Some may throw themselves into a career or hobby of some sort; others may experiment with drugs, alcoholism, or immorality. Still others will begin experimenting with occult or New Age spirituality. When we understand that people are longing for spiritual truth, we may be better able to empathize with those who have become involved in the occult.

It may come as a surprise to some to learn that *many* occultists have a Christian background. The problem is they oftentimes have been given the wrong impression of God or had some sort of negative experience in a church. It is heartbreaking to hear people recount stories of being beaten by nuns and forced to recite religious mantras. Obviously such experiences are not a reflection of true Christianity (neither experientially or doctrinally), but we need to be mindful that past hurts and doctrinal misunderstandings may be preventing occult followers from knowing what Christianity really is. A good way of clearing up some of these misconceptions is to simply *ask* how the person would define a Christian.

Many people think being a Christian simply means doing good works or attending a church. They need to know that a Christian is someone who has developed a personal relationship with God by accepting Christ as his Savior. Sharing the truth while showing genuine love and concern will go a long way toward helping people know who Jesus really is.

Past hurts are not the only stumbling blocks people have to Christianity. If you take time to listen, you will find out what other concerns the person may have. As he begins to open up to you, be prepared to exercise patience and love as you respond to him. (I will discuss more on this later.)

Much of the literature occultists are exposed to is either indifferent toward Christianity or downright hostile to it. The first time I realized this was when I started reading books on witchcraft and spells as a teenager. Although I wasn't particularly concerned about Christianity, I remember being quite taken aback by the very critical tone some of these books took. I can recall thinking the author of one textbook of magic, known as a *magikal grimoire*, seemed to go out of his way to take digs at Christianity and the church at every opportunity.

In the twenty years since then I have read many books on the occult and have seen this theme continue in both lesser and greater extents. So we must be aware that people who read occult literature are being fed a very negative picture of Christianity much of the time. This picture is also repeated on the Internet through the thousands of occult-related websites out there. Often, the same things are said over and over in different ways, as if to reinforce the same ideas into the reader's mind.

COMMON CRITICISMS

At this point it may be worth highlighting just a few of the most common criticisms that occultists are likely to raise about Christianity. In this way we can anticipate what people in the occult may say to us and how we can respond.

QUICK FACTS ABOUT THE OCCULT

• Occultists define the occult as truth—a deeper, more profound truth than the visible facts science provides.

• The occult is built upon one word: experience.

• Experience is not subject to divine authority.

• Death is not a violent result of sin; it has no sting, and it is neither friend nor enemy.[1]

Christians have perpetrated injustices in God's name

One of the most common objections raised against Christianity concerns the many injustices that have been done in God's name throughout the centuries, such as the Crusades and the sectarian violence that occurred in Northern Ireland. Especially distressing to practicing occultists (witches and Wiccans in particular) is the period of history often referred to as the dark ages, which pagans call "the burning times." During this terrible period in church history basically *anyone* who was perceived as being different in some way was dealt with most harshly.

Those who were vocal in disagreeing with the leaders of the church were branded as either heretics or witches and put to death by being drowned, burned at the stake, or hung. It cannot be denied that these terrible things happened in God's name by people professing Christianity. It is, therefore, easy to sympathize with the anger many pagans feel against the church due to that unfortunate chapter in history. However, certain vital facts need to be stressed.

Firstly and most importantly, it is highly unlikely that those who were killing in God's name were true Christians. The very fact that a church or individual labels itself "Christian" does not automatically mean they are a true follower of Jesus Christ, no matter who he or she may be. At various times throughout Christian history, evil and unregenerate men have infiltrated the established church and caused it to fall into apostasy. In fact, it should not surprise us that evil men masquerading as Christians will come and attempt to discredit and bring shame upon the message of Jesus Christ, as this is exactly what the Bible warns us would happen (2 Cor. 11:13, 26; Gal. 2:4; 2 Pet. 2:1–3; 1 John 3:15).

Genuine Christianity does not seek to harm its neighbor, but rather to do good to all by obeying the words of Christ, which state: "You shall love your neighbor as yourself" (Mark 12:31, NKJV). Those who are truly Christians have had a life-changing experience with Jesus Christ and would certainly seek to distance themselves from all violence, hate, and persecution of others. In fact, the Bible teaches that one who murders another does not have God's gift of eternal life within him (1 John 3:15).

Secondly, a lot of witches may be surprised to know that *other Christians*, not conforming to the corrupt established church of the day, were also put to death—and in great numbers! This is even acknowledged by Wiccan authorities.[2]

During times when the established church became apostate and corrupt, true followers of Christ often separated themselves and went underground while staying true to the teachings of Jesus. Many times during such difficult periods in history genuine believers were severely persecuted. But, again, those who persecuted both pagans and believers were unlikely genuine Christians themselves, but rather corrupt and evil men who took the opportunity to infiltrate the established church for their own selfish gain.

Christians are hypocritical

As I mentioned earlier, a number of people who are involved in the occult may have had bad experiences with churches or professing Christians. However, it may be worth mentioning two key points regarding this.

First, as I have said before, not everyone who calls himself a Christian is actually a follower of Christ. People attend church for various reasons; not everyone attending church is there to learn how to be more like Jesus. It is easy to focus on such individuals and paint everyone in the congregation with the same brush, but that would be unfair. This brings me to the second point: even those who *are* genuine Christians are by no means perfect (something we all will readily admit). Christians still have a sin nature that, sadly, causes us to fail at times.

Many pagans and Wiccans point to the sins of the church or individuals they may know whose Christian walk is less than exemplary and use this as justification to turn away from following Jesus Christ. Sadly, because of this, many have missed Jesus altogether. The Bible never tells us to fix our eyes on what the church is or is not doing. It tells us to "fix our eyes on Jesus, the author and perfecter of our faith" (Heb. 12:2).

The church is patriarchal

Due to the emphasis on the feminine and the goddess in modern-day paganism (Wicca and witchcraft especially), many involved in the occult claim that Christianity sees women as second-class citizens while viewing men as superior. They object to God being addressed as Father and the use of male pronouns when referring to God.

Although it can be said that Christians certainly do refer to God in masculine terms, this does not mean God is a male human being. Mormonism may teach this, but this is not Christian belief, and it never has been. In fact, the Bible specifically states that God is not a man (Hosea 11:9) but rather a Spirit (John 4:24). So why does the Bible refer to God in male terms?

In the Jewish culture at the time of Scripture, men did indeed carry the authority in both social and religious arenas. This is simply the order God instituted. Therefore, when God referred to Himself in masculine terms and believers called Him "Father," people in that time understood that His name was linked with His authority. This does not mean that God is a male human being. Any words we could use to address the omniscient, omnipresent, omnipotent, eternal God would be inadequate. But if we didn't ascribe personal terms to Him, then we would have to address Him as an "it," and this would not be in line with the personal nature of God as clearly revealed in the Bible.

Women are not second-class citizens in God's kingdom. It may come as a surprise to some, but Christianity was actually way ahead of the larger society in empowering women and affirming their value. Women often accompanied Jesus during His ministry, something few Jewish rabbis would have allowed at that time (Mark 15:40–41; Luke 8:1–3), and He frequently interacted with women who were not part of His immediate circle of followers, something that also was most unusual for a Jewish rabbi in that day (Matt. 15:21–28; Mark 7:24–30, 14:3–9; John 4:1–42, 12:1–8).

Women played a prominent role at Jesus's crucifixion (Matt. 27:55) and were the first to witness His resurrection (Matt. 28:1–10). In the early church women were prophetesses (Acts 21:9) and leaders such as deacons (*diakonos*: Rom. 16:1), and the apostle Paul referred to various women as coworkers in the gospel (Rom. 16:3;

Phil. 4:2–3). Jesus valued women. He did not, and does not, oppress them.

The Bible isn't trustworthy

Other common objections occultists raise include the trustworthiness of the Bible. Many feel it has been tampered with and that the church removed concepts such as reincarnation. Much has been written about the reliability of the Bible. (I highly recommend *A General Introduction to the Bible* by Norman Geisler and William E. Nix.[3]) Whenever I encounter this argument, I stress the reliability of the text and the vast amount of manuscript evidence for the New Testament, which is more than that of any other work of antiquity.

When challenged with this claim, I ask for hard evidence proving that concepts were taken out of the Bible. I explain that if this were the case, then we would find many ancient writings objecting to what the church had done. I also discuss good archeological examples that back up the Bible's claims, its prophecies, its accuracy in recounting geographical locations, and how it speaks factually about scientific issues. Again, there are many good Christian sources you can obtain to learn more about these topics.

A Spiritual Battle

Along with the many objections occultists have toward Christianity and the church, another barrier preventing them from turning to Christ are the very real spiritual forces at work in many of their lives. The last thing a demonic spirit wants is for an occultist to hear the gospel and allow the truth to set them free. So it should be no surprise that there may be a spiritual clash from time to time. This is why trusting in Christ and allowing the Holy Spirit the freedom to do His work is so important. We can learn only so many evangelism techniques. The Holy Spirit will show us exactly what we need to do. As we approach people involved in occultism, we must remember the importance of prayer and our total dependence on God.

To illustrate this, many years ago I stood outside a psychic fair with a couple of other Christian friends to chat with people walking by. After a while two women came out of one of the buildings screaming at us in a very aggressive manner. It soon became apparent that they were two of the mediums who had been giving readings at the fair. As the women spoke to us, I became aware of a man who had also come out of the building standing off to the side. He singled me out and told me I was "going to get a beating if we didn't disappear"! It turned out that he was the event's organizer and was angry that we were putting off the paying customers.

The situation was getting very ugly as the mediums continued to argue with us so loudly we could barely get a word in edgewise. While all this was going on, I became aware that the organizer had angrily stormed back inside the building for some reason (which was soon to become apparent). In the natural it seemed like a bad state of affairs to be in, so I quietly prayed, asking God to calm the women down and inviting Him in to be in control of the situation. Almost instantly the women grew calm and began listening to us. Their facial expressions softened, and something seemed to lift from them.

The heavy and oppressive atmosphere shifted and became calm. Something caught my eye again, and I saw that the man who had threatened me with a beating was headed toward us from across the parking lot. In his hand he had a large glass of water, which I assume he had planned to throw at us. He looked angry, but when he saw the contrast in the atmosphere, he seemed speechless and confused.

We were all chatting calmly and honestly together, laughing and sharing a joke! He listened for a while then turned and stormed back across the parking lot into the building. We left the mediums on a positive note, and everyone shook hands before we left. Later on when my friends and I discussed what had happened, we discovered that we all had been silently praying about the situation. We felt this is why we witnessed such an incredible turnaround.

Prayer is a vital instrument when we approach those involved in occultism. It is not an additional tool but a vital part of our preparation for evangelism. It is so crucial because we are up against invisible, evil spiritual entities that cannot be dealt with through natural means. All of the evangelistic techniques and theories in books can take us only so far in our witnessing.

Ultimately it is dependence upon the work of the Holy Spirit that really counts. We need to be aware that those who are engaged in occultism have opened themselves up to the very real risk of being influenced, controlled, and in some cases even possessed by demonic spirits, which are hostile to God and the message of the gospel. Depending on Christ and allowing oneself to be sensitive to the Holy Spirit is therefore essential.

The Right Attitude

As a final note, I want to mention another vital ingredient that will help us minister to those in pagan communities: love. Of course, this is necessary in our dealings with all people, no matter who they are. The problem is that many Christians know they should love others but sometimes fail to actually model that in their lives. Jesus said we are to be like salt and light to those in darkness (Matt. 5:13–16). In order to have this kind of influence, we must show people that we are genuinely interested in them and their concerns. People will quickly realize if we are putting on a good Christian façade.

I want to stress something here: showing love to occultists does not mean we compromise our beliefs. Sadly, a lot of people think it is unloving to challenge or criticize anyone's beliefs. They think we all should have a "live and let live" kind of attitude. These individuals typically fear being labeled "judgmental," "intolerant," or "unloving" if they challenge another person's faith in some way. But we must remember that Jesus challenged the religious views of His own day, and many of the New Testament epistles were written to counter false teaching that was circulating through the churches.

We can have effective and positive dialogue with those in the occult and various pagan groups. By simply setting boundaries and being clear about our beliefs, we engage in conversation with occultists without compromising our faith and falling into some sort of a mushy interfaith soup. In other words, although we are to have genuine love for those involved in occult practices and most certainly respect them, we must also be clear about why we disagree with their beliefs. We are to accept the person but not the practices. It is a fine line, and some Christians make the mistake of blurring the distinction, but it can be done. We can "love the sinner and hate the sin."

Disagreeing with someone doesn't mean arguing with him or allowing the conversation to degenerate into a heated debate. Certainly many dialogues of a religious or spiritual nature can get emotionally charged and tempers can flare. But the Bible clearly tells us that we are not to repay evil for evil or insult for insult (1 Pet. 3:9). Rather, we are to be self-controlled and polite, even to those who may be difficult. The Bible offers some sound advice in this area:

> The Lord's servant must not quarrel; instead, he must be kind to everyone, able to teach, not resentful. Those who oppose him he must gently instruct, in the hope that God will grant them repentance leading them to a knowledge of the truth, and that they will come to their senses and escape from the trap of the devil, who has taken them captive to do his will.
> —2 Timothy 2:24–26

When dialogue gets heated, remember the wise words from the Book of Proverbs: "A gentle answer turns away wrath, but a harsh word stirs up anger" (Prov. 15:1). If we maintain a calm and gentle manner in our dialogue with occultists (or anyone for that matter), we stand a better chance of diffusing a situation that may be getting intense. But if we become angry in return, we just add fuel to the fire, and the conversation will deteriorate. Even if we win the debate, that doesn't mean we will win that person over to Christ or even gain his respect or friendship.

I hope this chapter has offered some insight into the mind-set of occultists: why they think the way they do, what has led them to their conclusions about Christianity, and how Christians can respond. It is my prayer and hope that the body of Christ will become equipped and willing to build a bridge of understanding to those in the occult and show these lost ones a better way in their quest for spiritual truth. We need to sensitively let them know that the paths they are following will never satisfy, and all the things they are searching for can be found only in Jesus Christ. We do this "that they may know the mystery of God, namely, Christ, in whom are hidden all the treasures of wisdom and knowledge" (Col. 2:2–3).

RECOMMENDED RESOURCES

- *Freed From Satan's Grasp* by Vince McCann (Kingsway Communications, www .equippingthechurch.co.uk)

- *The Baptism of Boldness* by Walter Martin, CD/ audiotape (Walter Martin Ministries, www .waltermartin.com)

- *The Kingdom of the Occult* by Walter Martin, Jill Martin Rische, and Kurt Van Gorden (Thomas Nelson, 2008)

Vince McCann was led to occultism by a seemingly innocent fascination with paranormal phenomena such as ghosts and UFOs. Embracing the Gothic subculture further piqued his interest in dark forms of spirituality. Being slowly introduced to occult techniques and practices such as self-hypnosis, tarot cards, and white witchcraft, he began delving into darker aspects of the occult by acquiring a modern-day grimoire, or a textbook of magic, and calling directly on demons. All of this eventually brought him much torment at the hands of evil spirits until Jesus Christ dramatically intervened to bring salvation, deliverance, and healing. Vince is now dedicated to trying to help those who are involved in similar practices.

Chapter 9

DABBLING WITH DARKNESS

By Greg Griffin

THERE ARE MANY laws that govern the universe, both physical and spiritual. After dabbling in the occult for years, I found something to be universally true: involvement in witchcraft, Satanism, or any other form of the black arts will put you on a collision course with mental illness. Just think about it. God takes what little a person has, builds on it, and gives him hope. Satan, on the other hand, will take what little a person has in life and destroy it. Those of us who have been involved in darkness know this to be very true. But I am getting ahead of myself. Let me tell you how I came to this understanding.

I was adopted into a Christian home when I was three days old. My parents were loving and supportive. No abuse of any kind, trauma, domestic disturbances between my parents, or anything that would cause problems for a young kid. In fact, my parents tried their best to shelter me and give me the very best life they could.

My extended family was what you might call "normal" in the sense that they were all decent, hardworking, committed Christians. My family was not rich, but we had many blessings for which to be thankful. There is nothing in my upbringing that clearly explains how I ended up on a road to the occult. All I can say is that when I was around five years old, my family relocated from Texas to Colorado because my dad got a new job. And the move may not have been the cause, but that is when something clearly changed. I began to feel very alone and vulnerable for the first time in my life, and this made me long for a power that could protect me.

Even at such a young age I knew I was not a tough kid, and I was already struggling with feelings of rejection because my birth parents had given me up. I wanted to avoid ever being hurt again. This kind of emotional pain is so common among people in the occult. People are never drawn into the occult because they are on top of the world and all is well in their little universe. Across the board, those who search out power from the occult are hurting, lonely, and afraid in many areas of their lives.

Although I was adopted into a Christian family, I just did not think Jesus was what I needed. I can't explain exactly why I felt that way at only six years old. People are generally drawn to the light or the darkness, and I loved the darkness. Instead of being fun-loving and carefree, I became fascinated with ghosts, graveyards, and the like. I dwelt on death.

One day in 1975 a friend invited me to his house, and in his basement were a Ouija board and tarot cards. We consulted the Ouija board, and my friend's older sister read my tarot. Little did I know, I had just been initiated into the occult.

You might be thinking, "Wait a minute! All you did was play with some stupid game and get your future read." Of course, I didn't understand what I was getting myself into back then, but now I know. They aren't silly games to Satan. He will take whatever we will give him. By dabbling in the occult even as a "game," we step on the devil's turf and in a sense tell God, "Hey, I want Satan more than You!" Games? Not hardly!

I spent the next several years in Colorado in torment. At school I always felt that I did not belong. It is interesting that people in the occult *always* feel like outcasts. Was I a cool kid? Hardly! I was fearful, depressed, and lonely. I constantly thought of death and suicide. I felt my life was going downhill fast—not something you would expect to hear from a first-grader.

Around this time a couple of events occurred that made me even more fearful than I already was. First, some thugs in the neighborhood tried to kidnap me, then I started being bullied daily at school. I knew the things I dabbled in were dark, but I believed I needed them to survive. I felt powerless to keep bad things from happening to me, and I was tormented by fear.

In a child's foolish attempt to find some kind of power to protect me, I tried to give my life to evil and Satan. My thought was, "If I am evil, I will be protected." So I began to blaspheme God's name in made-up rituals. In my childish way I tried to worship death. I attempted to contact ghosts, though I had no idea how to make that happen. And I was driven to hurt myself by throwing myself into desks and chairs and hitting myself.

When I was around eight years old, my parents took me to a child psychologist. I was anxious and having panic attacks, and I could not sleep at all. I also cried all the time. My parents and this counselor did not fully understand why I acted the way I did. They knew about the bullying and the kidnapping attempt, but they didn't know about the Ouija board or the tarot cards or the attempts to summon the dead. After some Freudian mumbo-jumbo and action steps for my parents, we were sent on our way, but nothing the psychiatrist recommended made much difference. I continued to walk around crying, never talking to people, and having nightmares.

A year later when my dad took another new job, I found myself in North Carolina in a fourth-grade class. At least seven students shared each table. To my amazement all of the students assigned to my table were fascinated with witchcraft, sorcery, and the dead. In the years since then I have found that people who dabble in the occult seem to attract others like them. If they move, they will usually find others interested in the dark arts within the first week or so of relocating. In talking with numerous people who have come out of the occult, I have found this to be consistently the case.

After a few months of getting to know these kids, I recognized a commonality: we were all paranoid in one way or another. These classmates of mine admitted that they were afraid of spirits attacking them, just as I was. (For some odd reason I had always been afraid of demons taking over my body.) My friends and I weren't just youth struggling with depression and wild imaginations. No matter what normal struggles we may have been facing, if my friends and I had not spent so much time filling our minds with dark, evil thoughts, our lives would have been much different.

Throughout elementary school I constantly researched spirits, UFOs, Satan, demons, and the paranormal in the libraries of the schools I attended. Just about all the music I listened to was talking about hell and death. Although I was still quite young, many days I would come home and put a knife to my wrist, wanting to kill myself but never actually allowing the knife to cut my skin. I would have fits of beating myself, trying to hurt myself in any way I could, all of which I hid from my parents.

Moving to Kansas with my family was the surprise I received in seventh grade. I decided to stop hitting myself—new school, new life. The self-beating stopped, but some things didn't change. A few days into my seventh-grade year I met some boys who, like me, were outcasts and fascinated with the occult. We spent long afternoons playing Dungeons and Dragons, and we talked for hours about the joys of suicide, thrasher films, and all things weird and dark.

I remember thinking at the time that if I became truly evil, I would have all the things I wanted in life—most importantly, no one would ever be able to hurt me again. I also remember hating Christians. I thought to myself while mowing the lawn one day, "I wish we could gather up all the Christians in America and kill them!" The real problem was not the Christians but their Savior. Being in a Christian family and always finding myself around Christians, I was deeply offended by the gospel. I thought, "I will never bow to God or Christ!" I thought Christians were all losers, but the real loser was me.

The Christians I knew were full of peace, hope, and joy. My pals and I were the tormented ones. When I talk about my time in the occult, I find myself using the word *torment* a lot. That is because when one practices the black arts in any way, the result will be internal torment. This torment is a combination of deep, turbulent emotions—the fear of death and of life, as well as hurt and pain caused by life circumstances.

All people experience sad and difficult times, but the addition of evil philosophies, hatred, and a fascination with suicide, death, divination, and the like will quickly make matters much worse. The normal pain everyone experiences is compounded by the guilt, hopelessness, and despair the occult brings into a person's life. This horrible emotional cocktail can make a person lose the will to live, and Satan is well on his way to destroying yet another soul. Tragic!

FINDING CHURCH BUT NOT JESUS

My high school years are kind of a blur. At age fifteen, I had what one might say was a nervous breakdown. I had panic attacks and was eventually diagnosed with bipolar disorder. Obsessive thoughts raced through my mind continually. After seeing a psychiatrist, I was administered a series of medications. The doctor wanted to help, but I was a mess.

In high school I finally found what I thought were some really cool friends. They were a combination of drug dealers, gang members, and street fighters. I'd hit the big time now (just kidding, of course!). My best friend was the leader of a gang called Satan's Saints. He was a tough guy, or so I thought. I thought my buddies were so cool and wicked. Inside they were as frightened as I was. This is another truth about people in the occult. They aspire to be powerful, but they are scared kids inside, longing to be loved and accepted. Don't let their spells, magic, worship of Satan, or evil acts fool you. They are really in turmoil.

After much introspection I realized what my involvement with the occult was doing to me. Several of my friends had committed suicide. Others had fried their brains on LSD. And I began to see how depraved I was becoming. All I wanted to do was hurt people in my heart, and I could not feel happy, joyful, or peaceful. Worse, I felt I could not love people.

I began to attend church with a searching heart. A few months later I made a profession of faith, but I had no idea what I was doing, and my life changed very little. A lot of people who've been in the occult look for God but, like me, get involved in religion without really discovering who Jesus is. It is important when witnessing to someone in the occult that you make sure he or she understands sin, the cross, and salvation. So many people want God but instead end up joining a religious system that will not give them hope or the new life they desire.

After high school there was college and frequent hospitalizations throughout my twenties. I wanted to die many times. Still haunted by all the darkness in my past, I felt socially anxious and frightened to be with groups of people. Although I went to church, I was always confused about what was really true, so I hadn't found peace in a relationship with Christ. I tried to believe in Jesus, but I did not understand how God could become a man or how anyone could actually rise from the dead. Deep inside, I questioned it all.

I bumped into people all the time who were involved in witchcraft and the occult, and I began picking up on a common theme. Many of them wanted to die or kill themselves. I find it interesting that many Christians are afraid of people in the occult because they think they are "violent and powerful." But if they are so "powerful," why do they want to kill themselves? Is that the fruit of being truly powerful?

There is a measure of power in the occult. This is true. But that so-called power comes with torment, anxiety, and depression. All power from the occult ultimately ends in despair and death, and these people perish without hope!

Beyond suicide, there are many other practices common among those in the occult that are equally pointless and stupid. When I would have periods of extreme sadness, I would cut myself with a razorblade to appease the being I viewed as God. When I was cutting I felt relief, like I had somehow atoned for my sins. I reasoned that if I hurt myself and drew blood, good things would happen to me.

Many in the occult practice some form of self-mutilation. Add to that drugs, alcohol, and sexual perversion, and it's easy to see that occultists are on a dangerous path. It's amazing. God sacrificed His own Son for us while Satan wants people to sacrifice themselves for him. What a contrast!

I will never forget the time I was admitted to a psychiatric hospital in North Carolina. I was twenty-one years old. The admitting nurse read in my file that I had dabbled in the occult. She looked at me and said, "Greg, you are in no way the first person to come to this hospital who has been in the occult." I later found out that psychiatric wards are filled with people who sought power through the occult and ended up weak, hopeless, and broken.

Although in some ways my life started getting better during my twenties, I was continually searching for something I could not quite put my finger on. I would attend church at times, but in my heart I didn't know what I longed for. At the church I attended in college, I was involved in a lot of volunteer ministry because I wanted to help people who were hurting. I knew from experience exactly how that felt. The church members often commended me for my volunteer work and encouraged me to attend seminary. So, thanks to the generosity of the church and my denomination, I enrolled in seminary after I graduated from college.

Here I was, someone who had dabbled in the occult trying to understand serious spiritual truths while still dealing with major life issues myself. The seminary professors did not help my anxiety at all. I was seeking ultimate truth, and my professors told me the Bible was full of contradictions and errors. I was told the God Christians worshipped could have been a pagan god invented by Abraham's tribe and then later exalted by Abraham because he felt afraid. When my seminary studies came to a close, I went off to chaplain's school, where I ran into many of the same beliefs. I was taught that the Bible and Christianity were great but not entirely true. One could pick and choose what he wanted to believe. To say this was not helpful in my search for truth would be an understatement.

When people exit the occult, they always search. Some will get involved in a religious institution trying to be "good" people. They will attempt to balance the cosmic scale of right and wrong yet still struggle with the issues they have always known. Like me, many end up in Christian churches but still have absolutely no concept of the true God. Let me be very clear on this matter: after someone has been hurt and nearly destroyed by occult principles and practices, even someone like me who just dabbled (I was never a priest of witchcraft or a high-ranking coven member), the only hope is truly knowing God through Jesus. Religion cannot help; positive thinking cannot help; education cannot help; dating a hot guy or girl cannot help; money cannot help, nor can any material thing.

The only thing that can change a heart nearly destroyed by the occult is a relationship with Jesus. And which Jesus would that be? After all, there are many takes on Christ, are there not? There is the Gnostic Jesus, who was visited by the Christ spirit; the Mormon Jesus, who is brother to Lucifer; or even the nice-guy Jesus of liberalism, who just went around loving people and doing good. None of these will suffice for a heart ripped apart by Satan. The Jesus I am testifying about is the divine Son of God. Almighty God in human form, born of a virgin, the One who died for our sins and physically rose from the dead—He is the only way and only hope for people like me.

How did I finally meet this Jesus? At age forty, on April 3, 2009, I realized that I did not know for sure what I believed. At approximately 1:00 a.m. that day I was honest with God. I simply asked, "God, is Jesus really Your Son, and did He rise from the dead, or is this just mythology?"

I suddenly began thinking of the Ten Commandments. When I measured my life against God's standards, I realized I had broken all of the commandments in some way or another. In God's eyes if you hate, you have murdered. If you lust, you have committed adultery. Then for reasons I can't fully explain, all of the Messianic prophecies about Jesus made sense to me, and as this happened, I came to the understanding that Jesus is God and that He is risen. This was coupled with an awareness of God's love and power. I knew in my heart that without Jesus I would go to hell. That early morning Jesus became God to me—my Lord and Savior! I now know in my heart that He is real.

True knowledge of Christ comes when we as sinners acknowledge we need a Savior and that we need God's help in our daily lives. It comes as we turn from our sins the best we know how and trust Jesus to save us. In other words, we admit to God: "I need You. Save me!" Proverbs 3:34 says, "Though He [God] scoffs at the scoffers, yet He gives grace to the afflicted" (NAS). God will always have mercy on those who admit they are weak and needy. That's not something strong and proud people want to acknowledge and surely not something someone serving the devil will want to admit!

Is life a bed of roses now? Not at all, but things are different in many ways. Being sure that Jesus is real gives me a new perspective. It is like the blinders have come off for good. I still have sad and anxious times, but it is different now. In the occult I felt on my own because I was alienated from God. Now I know I'm never alone, because I truly believe Jesus's promise in Hebrews 13:5 that He will never leave me or forsake me. I look at it this way: Jesus died alone, forsaken by God for our sins. When we trust Him, we never have to be alone again. His Spirit dwells in our hearts.

TWO RULES OF THE OCCULT

We see movies about satanic worship, witchcraft, and all the supposed awesomeness of being part of the occult. Spells, vampirism, black magic, and charms fill the pages of young peoples' fantasy books these days. But is that really what sums up thousands of years of the occult, witchcraft, and all that the black arts represent?

Not at all. I have found that occult followers live by two funda-
mental rules:

1. Do what thou wilt, for this is the whole of the law.

2. Say in your heart, I am my own redeemer.

The first rule was espoused by a man named Aleister Crowley, an
influential occultist who lived in the early twentieth century. The
second was written in *The Satanic Bible* by Anton Szander LaVey.
As I expound on the effects of these two commands from Satan,
you will see why I say the occult leads to mental illness and torment.

Crowley was an occultist with ties to a magical society called
the Golden Dawn. Some consider him one of the most influential
occultists of all times, and it saddens me to know he came from
a devout Christian family and his father was a minister. In 1904
Crowley claimed to have received a text known as *The Book of the
Law* from a supposedly divine source. He used this text to develop
an occult philosophy called Thelema, which espoused the rule "Do
what thou wilt."

Doing "what thou wilt" simply means going your own way in
life—rejecting God's love and gift of Jesus, and deciding to do life
by your own rules. Anyone who lives life on his own terms is practicing a satanic philosophy.

Crowley left all forms of Christianity to prove to himself and the
world just how wonderful he was. When one gets involved in the
things of Satan, one bears the fruit of Lucifer, the one who rebelled
against God. The occult is all about pride. Pride is saying, "God, I
know better how to live my life than You do!" Isaiah 53:6 reads, "All
we like sheep have gone astray, each of us has turned to his own
way" (NAS). Isn't it interesting that the rebellion spoken of in the
Bible is identical to life in the occult? First Samuel 15:23 even says
rebellion is as the sin of witchcraft.

The second law is that we are our own saviors, which, as I mentioned, is written in *The Satanic Bible*. The true Bible says we are

all sinners and in need of salvation. Not only do we need the blood of Jesus to wash away our sins and shame, but we also need God to help and protect us in this evil world. Again, humility leads one to cry out, "God, I need help. I cannot save or help myself. I am utterly in need of You in every way."

The satanic way proclaims, "God, I can handle my life on my own. I will be able to save myself by my own strength, power, brains, and effort. God, go away! I have it all under control." This attitude totally disregards all that God has done. It is an absolute rejection of God's plan and grace through Jesus.

These two commandments can be seen throughout occult literature historically because at the root of the occult is humanism. Humanism is the exaltation of man or woman and the worship of the created rather than the Creator! It elevates self and degrades God. A lot of people think of the occult as devil worship, but not every occultist surrenders his will to Satan and tries to follow him. The truth is, anyone who chooses to thumb his nose at God and reject His love and sacrifice in an attempt to live his own life is worshipping a false god. They are saying, "I am all powerful and glorious. Look at me! I am God!" That attitude is a slap in the face to God.

Let's examine the fruit of this way of living—having a prideful attitude and dwelling on dark beliefs founded in the occult. Many who travel this path end up in a life filled with excesses—too much drinking, drugs, materialism, and self-exaltation. They do whatever they want. Crowley himself abused drugs and died in shame. Many have followed the same path. Living in this darkness leads to mental anguish and despair. Many in this state take their lives.

And though many people attempt to be their own savior, it is easy to see that we are not in control of our lives. Even the healthiest among us cannot control whether cancer invades their bodies. They can't stop the loss of the loved one or an economic downturn. Successful men and women have wound up homeless. Take it from me, anyone can be instantly humbled by God. Do not doubt this ever. I too once believed these commandments of Satan. Then I found myself broken with many physical ailments and suffering mentally and emotionally. Doing what thou wilt and living as though you are your own redeemer just do not work.

No Need to Fear

I have heard Christians testify to being afraid of witnessing to people involved in an occult-related belief system. Believe me: you have no need to be fearful! Many times these people are afraid of you! Why? You have the power they truly want. First John 4:4 says, "Greater is he that is in you, than he that is in the world" (KJV).

Even though occultists put up a front and claim to be fearless, most are frightened, broken, and lonely inside. That is my experience and that of others testifying in this book. Today I am forty-three years old. I battle severe physical illnesses and still have bouts with depression and anxiety from time to time. Sometimes life gets so overwhelming I even feel as if there is no hope. Then I recall that life is not about me but God. Hope returns when I focus on Jesus!

How different is my life now? Am I some guy with everything going for me? No way! The difference is this: I know God through Christ! It is that simple. Sometimes I still cry from a broken heart, and sometimes I am fearful and feel alone. We have all felt this way if we are honest! But the big difference between God's children and Satan's followers is that God's children have hope and someone with them who is almighty and all-powerful. And they know how it feels to be loved by God, the only One whose opinion matters anyway.

I know there are many Christians who are lonely too. Across America we hear of Christians who struggle day to day with loneliness because they are divorced, widowed, single parents, or perhaps never married. I know how this feels. I have never been married and live by myself in a small town. But because I have God's Spirit residing in me, I am compelled to reach out to others. God helps me to reach out to hurting people even when I feel the pains of loneliness myself. He changes my outlook and gives me hope, joy, and contentment. He is the key to everything.

I want to close with a few words about how Christians can reach out to someone involved in the occult in an effective way. Let's begin by reviewing some of the principles we have discussed thus far.

Lead with the fact that we are all searching for something.

Occultists, vampire fanatics, witches, etc. are all searching for power to keep from being destroyed by this cruel world. Many of us were on the same search when we came to Christ. A pagan might not be able to articulate it, but he struggles with all the things you struggle with: What is the meaning of life? Why am I here? And ultimately they long for the same hope you have found. They want to know how to fill the void inside. You know the truth; share it!

Let them know the seriousness of sin.

Explain that we all deserve hell and judgment from God; then share from God's Word the remedy: a relationship with Jesus Christ! The occultist needs to understand that he cannot be good enough or be his own savior. Only Jesus can save us; we cannot save ourselves!

Remember the realities of heaven and hell.

Here is a key to consider when witnessing to people involved in the occult: they are already in hell in so many ways! They are being tormented inside their hearts. Address the pain and hurt they feel. At first they will deny how they feel and put up a bold front. Just know it is a façade. After a while they usually will crack and break down in tears. They are looking for comfort and hope. Who is the great physician in your life? How has Jesus calmed the storm in your heart? Be bold and share this with these struggling people. God is with you in this.

Do not be afraid.

In all I have discussed about witnessing, I hope you recognize a theme: you don't have anything to fear. Granted, you must use discernment. Don't go out ministering alone, and do not confront violent people. But do not be afraid of being cursed or hexed. Make sure you are prayed up and being led by the Holy Spirit. In other words, when taking on the task of witnessing to people bound by the occult, stay close to God! This is good advice anyway, right?

I suppose one of the major lessons I have learned is that we all want to be accepted and to fit in. I see it even in churches, people trying to be part of the right cliques and run with the right crowd. The real question is, does God accept us? And the answer is undeniably yes. If God accepts us, that is more important than fitting into a clique.

I would love to think all churches would be loving and open toward anyone who walks through the doors. But my experience tells me this is not always the case. It is possible even for those with the best of intentions to overlook a visitor or new member. I believe God wants the church, His body, to be His hands and feet and minister to others in love and compassion. I also believe the main reason to attend church is to worship God, so I always encourage people, especially those coming from an occult background, to push past any feelings of isolation and find a place to serve.

I have found this to be the big dividing line between Satan's kingdom and God's kingdom. In God's kingdom we still struggle with all sorts of issues and problems. But in Christ's kingdom His children live to serve others. Someone who is of the devil serves only himself. He has a me-me-me attitude. People who serve will tell you that even though they may struggle mentally and emotionally, when they get their minds off themselves and onto serving others, they get better quickly. Serving others in love gives you a sense of purpose and meaning in life.

This is the result of following Jesus: a heart that wants to serve. Jesus stressed the importance of serving others repeatedly—because it honors Him and changes lives. I've been self-centered and selfish Satan's way. I also know how it feels to do things God's way and find places to serve. And let me tell you, serving is an incredible way to live!

These two ways—the way of self and the way of Christ—are always available to everyone in this world. Following our own way leads to death; following God's way leads to life. Deep down, I think people even in the occult know this truth.

Believe it or not, people in the occult want deep down to make a difference in others' lives. Someone who has abandoned the occult for Christ might be confused as to how to get started, but you can show him the way.

I also want to say to the Christians reading this book that people involved in the occult may not be who you think they are. Many are smart and well educated, have good jobs, and are materially successful. They are very often sensitive, caring, and compassionate. The sad thing is, when a person serves the devil, those good emotions are replaced by hatred and fear and pain. With Jesus, they can find them again and begin to fulfill God's purposes.

FINDING THE WAY HOME

It takes time to find your way back to a normal life after being in the occult and putting all those dark beliefs in your head. But what major life change doesn't? Look at recovering drug addicts. They must learn to live without drugs. Anyone in recovery of any kind— be it for alcoholism or the traumas of war—must learn how to start anew. It's the same with occult recovery.

Many people come to faith in Christ and think some magic wand will be waved over them, and all will be OK. But genuine healing doesn't work that way. When I came out of the occult then truly found Jesus at age forty, I experienced a season of trials, brokenness, crushing, and remolding by God. I went through some of the most painful times I've ever had in my life. But I found this truth along the way: Satan *likes* to hurt us; he wants to kill, steal, and destroy. But when God breaks us, it is for our own good! God has to get all the dross and evil out of us. The process is not pleasant, to be sure, but He only allows us to go through that kind of difficulty because He knows it will bless us.

I think it is truly amazing that with God, the broken times, the painful days when we cry and are crushed, help us to grow and gain strength. For the Satanist, those times do not have any redeeming value. Over and over, even in the darkest days, God can bring good out of anything. How about witches? Do their pagan gods promise that good will come out of their dark times? Yet Romans 8:28 tells the child of God that all things will work for the good in our lives. What a difference!

Today I have learned that when I am weak, then I am truly strong because of Christ. I now can admit my weaknesses and faults and bring them to God in prayer. I always look for opportunities to share Jesus with people, and I try to encourage the hurting and sick. My dreams of being a rich, famous big shot with all the power I once craved are gone forever. I am now happy to be a regular guy with a lot of problems that I daily bring before the Lord so He can help me grow and be more like Jesus.

In time I realized God could use all the suffering I went through for His glory, and I have been blessed to share His love with people in nursing homes, my community hospital, and even a support group for the mentally ill. I am convinced that has made the biggest difference in my life! I see now that what matters most in life is glorifying God and serving Him.

Nothing is more significant, and nothing brings more satisfaction. Even when I was in seminary, I wanted to be a successful minister and climb the ladder to fame and glory. I see now that was just Satanism under a different guise. I was still worshipping the power and fame that could be found in this world. I serve God today because I know He is real, and I know I truly need Him.

It is sad that it took me forty years to figure all this out, but better late than never, I guess. I do not know what lies ahead for me. But I know having a relationship with Jesus has changed everything.

I started this chapter by saying God builds on what little we give Him, and Satan takes away the little we have and destroys us. I hope you can see this is true. I have seen Jesus put so many broken people back together again that it is astounding. Jesus is the great healer and gives hope to the hopeless.

I still have two commandments I live by today, but they are different from the rules I followed when I was dabbling in the occult. The change in my life and mental well-being are because of these two guiding principles. What are they?

1. Do what thou will, My God and Savior! Not my will, but Yours be done.

2. Jesus, You are my Savior and Redeemer!

Those two principles will change your life just as they did mine! The same Savior who died for us two thousand years ago is with us today. He is the source of every good thing in life. I want people in the occult to find Jesus—and soon. But they need someone to tell them of His love and power. I know it is difficult at times to know what to say when witnessing. If we put our lives in His hands, He will give us the right words. I will go out and share Jesus. Will you?

Greg Griffin writes Christian music and performs at churches. He earned a master's of divinity degree from Southwestern Baptist Theological Seminary and ministers through chaplaincy programs as well as in nursing homes and support groups for the mentally ill.

Chapter 10

DEMON POSSESSION—A MOTHER'S STORY

By Carol Carlson

A LTHOUGH RAISED IN an atheistic family, I spoke to God. I believed in my heart that He had to be real. In my late teens and early twenties I followed many paths looking for Him. They seemed OK at first, because whether it was spiritualism, numerology, Scientology, the paranormal, or psychic Edgar Cayce's enlightenment teachings, they all quoted the Bible and claimed some regard for Jesus. (Spiritualists called Him a medium; numerologists said He practiced numerology, but they acknowledged Him as a great teacher.)

However, each experience with the occult only scared the wits out of me. I began to drink heavily and ended up in a tormented and suicidal state. I was in that condition when a friend invited me to her church and I heard the gospel message for the first time. While sitting in the church service, I heard a voice speak to my heart, "This is it, the truth you have been looking for."

My husband was not a Christian, but I raised our four children to know Jesus as their Savior too. At one point I was even a little smug, as my two older girls married Christian men and my two younger kids, Scott and Chris, were active in church and Bible study. Then the two younger ones entered high school, and things changed.

My teenagers fell in with a group of troubled youth from an alternative school nearby. The new friends wore all black and had purple hair. The girls had pasty white powdered faces punctuated with bright red lipstick. They all had numerous body piercings.

179

Scott assured me these new friends were not dangerous, just different. But my curiosity led me to read Chris's diary, and I was horrified by what I read: "Scott and I snuck out of the house last night and met Amy and Bo at the cemetery. Bo brought some pot. At midnight, we lit candles and used a Ouija board. I didn't get any answers, but Amy did. Amy scares me. She told me she is a witch. Once, she stopped walking with me and told me to not look, as she sometimes gets possessed and falls down. She said I should ignore it, as she never knows when it will happen."

Marijuana? Witchcraft? Both Scott and Chris knew better! I had taught them how the Bible called such practices detestable to God (Deut. 18:10–12, Isa. 8:19–20). After I confessed that I had read the diary, I told them that as Christians, they must walk with those who are in the light, not those who are in the dark. Chris seemed to listen, but Scott did not. I learned that in addition to pot, he was using LSD and PCP and drinking alcohol. Our youth pastor met with him, and I held endless discussions with him, but to no avail.

My son shut himself in his room and wrote poems about suicide. In my own diary I paraphrased a verse from Psalm 107:10–11: "He sits in darkness and deepest gloom...for he has rebelled against the Word of God. He is becoming a fool because of his rebellious ways."

I was encouraged, however, when Scott's dad and I decided to move to the Pacific Northwest, where I grew up and where he supposedly planned to retire. I thought the move to a more rural area would cause Scott and Chris to exchange their bad friends for good ones, but they only sought out the same kind. Black clothing. Mohawk haircuts. Teardrop tattoos on their cheeks. One guy wore a long cape.

My husband was with us in our new home for only two weeks before he returned to California, and I learned that he had left us for good. I became a suddenly single mom with a teenage son whose drug use had escalated to crystal meth and "shrooms," or psychedelic mushrooms. Once after being gone all night, he stumbled in and told me he'd had a terrifying trip on acid laced with strychnine and speed and thought he was going to die. I thought the bad trip would scare him away from ever using drugs again, but it didn't.

DRUGS, DEMONS, AND THE PSYCH WARD

I drew closer to the Lord for strength, and He held my hand, counseling me on what to do day by day. One of His instructions was to attend a Tough Love parent support group. It was there that I met David, the single dad of a wayward daughter. Our support of each other turned to dating and, two years later, marriage. During those two years David helped me through more tough times, which included a five-day, out-of-control drug party that took place in my home when I visited my older daughters in California.

Scott eventually moved out of our house and into an old, rundown apartment he shared with friends. Early one morning a roommate called to tell me that my son had "totally lost it" and was in jail. When David and I raced over to Scott's apartment, he was in the back of a police car, waiting to be transported to the psychiatric unit of the local hospital. My wild-eyed son told me that cops were planning to kill him.

At the hospital a doctor told me Scott had a drug-induced psychosis but would be fine within a week. The psychiatric nurse on his ward said otherwise. "On weekends lots of kids end up here," she told us. "But it's more than drugs. There's a definite Satanic influence, and the staff knows it. They just don't know what to do about it."

David and I made regular visits to the hospital. On the way there one evening I found myself silently praying, "If this is some sort of demonic thing, please expose it and make it clear to me." God did. We found Scott more distressed than usual, pacing the floor, and clasping and unclasping his hands. We made small talk, but he interrupted us.

"I've been battling demons," he said. "Not imagined ones but the real thing. Last night I thought I would have to take on Lucifer himself."

"Was it a dream?" I asked.

"No. No. Not at all."

David spoke first, "If there are demons, Scott, you must resist. You have to pray to God for them to leave you alone."

"And you must have weapons to fight them with," I added. "You must know God's Word and how to be strong in Him."

But Scott rambled on that he couldn't pray because "the demons steal my identity." Nothing we said allayed his fears, and when I tried to give my son a hug, he backed away.

"Do you remember that verse, 'My name is Legion?'" he asked, referring to Mark 5:9.

Ignoring his question, I placed my hands on his shoulders and looked directly into his eyes, "Honey, it's going to be all right."

As soon as I spoke, Scott's head rolled back, his lips curled downward, and an ugly expression crossed his face. He began to moan.

"Oh, God," I whispered. "Help us."

His mouth opened wider, and his moans became louder. David would say later that the sounds were uncanny, as though air was just rushing past his windpipe. As Scott tried to move away from me, he nearly fell. Supporting his weight with one arm, I tried to calm him while praying, "Lord, help us. If it's demons, I pray in the mighty name of the Lord Jesus Christ that they will release this young man and leave him alone. I pray the blood of Jesus Christ over my son."

Then Scott crashed heavily to the floor, where he lay facedown and unconscious. David ran to his side and rolled him over. His mouth gaped open; his eyes were wide and staring. Saliva bubbled from his mouth. I thought he was dead. Nurses watched from the doorway, immobilized. I screamed, "*Do* something!"

One of them knelt next to him and said that his vitals were normal. With a stern look she demanded that we leave. Numbly we made our way to the waiting room. After a half hour a nurse pulled up a chair across from us. She said Scott was in a semiconscious state but doing OK—"Oh, and he keeps mumbling something about being released..."

When I arrived back at home, I called the hospital, and Scott was put on the line. "Hi, Mom!"

"Scott! How are you?"

"Better now, Mom. Thanks! Well, I got to go work on my clay jar now."

My tormented son was back and in his right mind. Hospital records that I obtained months later described the events this way: "Patient was visiting with mom. Shortly thereafter patient was observed lying on floor moaning and mother was conducting what appeared to be some type of exorcism."

The record goes on to say, "Patient…talked freely about demon leaving his body when mother prayed over him. He believes that was the main demon. He was appropriate and self-directed and looking forward to discharge."

David and I believed that evil had left Scott's body, but that night I asked God to confirm it. I opened my Bible at random to Psalm 34, and the first words that jumped out at me had to do with deliverance:

- "He delivered me" (v. 4).

- "He delivers them" (v. 7).

- "The righteous cry out, and the Lord hears them; he delivers them" (v. 17).

- "A righteous man may have many troubles, but the Lord delivers him from them all" (v. 19).

I had my answer. The next day I read an account of deliverance from demonic possession in Mark 9:17–27. A man had brought his son to Jesus because he was possessed by a spirit. When the spirit saw Jesus, it immediately threw the boy into a convulsion. The boy fell to the ground and rolled around, foaming at the mouth. The spirit shrieked and came out. The boy looked so much like a corpse that many said, "He's dead." I compared what I read with what had just happened to us. Although the spirit did not openly confront Jesus, it did confront Jesus *in me.*

As with the possessed boy in the Gospel of Mark, Scott had shrieked. Scott had fallen. Scott had foamed at the mouth. And, as with those looking at the possessed boy, I had thought he was dead. No matter. If it would take this for my son to commit his life to Jesus Christ, it would be well worth it. I could hardly wait for visiting hours and Scott's new beginning. But the battle had just begun.

In the Gospel of Matthew the Bible says, "When an evil spirit comes out of a man, it goes through arid places seeking rest and does not find it. Then it says, 'I will return to the house I left.' When it arrives, it finds the house unoccupied, swept clean and put in order. Then it goes and takes with it seven other spirits more wicked than itself, and they go in and live there. And the final condition of that man is worse than the first" (Matt. 12:43–45).

Scott's relief at being in his right mind did not last. He did not see how drugs and the occult had sent him to the hospital, nor did he thank God for releasing him from mental torment. Because his "house" was not occupied by the Holy Spirit, the door was open for the evil occupants to reenter.

QUICK FACTS ABOUT DEMON POSSESSION

- Satan is the power behind all occult psychic phenomena; his purpose is to deceive mankind and lead people away from God.
- The Bible teaches that demon possession is a common occurrence, not a rare phenomenon.
- Exorcism, used with care and concern, delivers people from evil and promotes healing.
- Jesus taught exorcism by example, and the church must follow His lead.
- One should never enter battle against the world of the occult without prayer.[1]

THIS PRESENT DARKNESS

Released from the hospital, Scott asked to live with us for a while. This sounded good, but one Sunday David and I returned from church to find no Scott. Hours later he stumbled out of the woods behind our house saying he had fallen asleep under a bush and didn't know where he was. He said, "When you are lost, you must stay put until found." Then he decided to walk to the west side of town, fifteen miles away. We could not stop him.

At four thirty the next morning the police picked him up again, this time for walking down the median of the freeway. Back to the psychiatric unit. Their diagnosis: "unspecified psychosis." Scott's former roommate called to tell me that while Scott was missing from home, he had come by his old apartment and left a note on the door that said, "Basil August Greyhand-Elvis Presley 4 or not. PS: Bells, bells—purple like—they're ringing in the ears."

It was happening again, only worse this time. I got on my knees and cried out, "Mighty God, I claim the power of Jesus Christ to release my son from every pretension that has set itself up against the knowledge of God" (2 Cor. 10:5). I prayed that Scott would be permanently restored to his right mind like the possessed man in Mark 5: "They saw the man who had been possessed by the legion of demons, sitting there, dressed and in his right mind" (v. 15).

The next ten days in the hospital proved that Scott's mind was in some other world, yet once again he was released to our care. One morning as Scott was sitting on the couch mumbling to himself, I mentioned to him that many people were praying for him. He answered, "Either I'm mentally ill or possessed." Then he added, "Mom, *do* get everyone to pray for me. Mother, are you going to cast demons out of me?"

Hope at last! I called our pastor, and he said after church on Sunday he would come with a group of friends to pray. It was only Thursday, and I hoped we could wait that long, especially when

Scott disappeared for another twenty-four hours and showed up at a college campus that was miles away.

We were unable to attend church that Sunday, but I expected a call from Pastor Jim. It didn't come. Scott became so out of control that David insisted he readmit himself to the hospital, and he agreed. I thought the indescribable pain would kill me. During my next day's visit I finally asked my son outright, "Do you think it was the drugs that put you back in this place?"

"No," he said.

"Then what do you think is going on?"

"I think..." he scrunched up his face, speaking with difficulty. "I think that...this present darkness is here. In me," he said, quoting from Frank Peretti's novel *This Present Darkness*. "But the doctor started me on Trilafon, and it's going to help." Scott smiled. Then he opened his *Metamagical Themas* book and shared his latest revelations.

Though the spiritual holds on my son were great, I determined to persevere in prayer until the battle was won. There is power when we pray in accordance to God's Word. So at home I opened my Bible and prayed several verses from Psalm 94: "Rise up, O Judge...pay back to Scott's enemies what they deserve, for how long will those wicked ones be jubilant over their victory? But You know! You will not reject him forever. You will take a stand and help him. You will become his fortress, his rock, and his refuge."

After two weeks in the hospital Scott developed a "Messiah complex," thinking he might be Jesus. Yet he was once again released to us. This time his caseworker arranged to have him stay at a motel where she could monitor him. I prayed from Psalm 57:1, "Have mercy on Scott, O God. Cause his soul to take refuge in You, in the shadow of Your wings until the disaster has passed. Send from heaven and save him!"

I visited my son daily, listening patiently as he told me about aliens and how he feared that his brain was bulging out of his skull. After a few weeks he was moved into an apartment, from where he would receive outpatient treatment. He put a can of Spam by the door to keep evil spirits away.

By now his psychiatrists had ruled out a drug-induced psychosis. The bizarre behaviors were lasting too long. Yet he did not fit the diagnosis of being schizophrenic or bipolar. They didn't know what was wrong with him, and had I suggested evil spirits, they would have committed *me*.

The drama continued. Scott's roommate and friends studied ceremonial magic. They drew pentagrams and chanted spells that would invite the presence of demons. He told me he could summon them at his bidding! To him they were a harmless power to be harnessed. He also began experimenting with pagan rituals, Zen Buddhism, Wicca, and witchcraft. And he hailed the merits of pot.

Along the way Scott fell in love with a girl named Lisa, and they moved into an apartment together. He was living on disability checks. She worked at a fast-food restaurant. I wrote letters saying God had once restored his mind, but he had rejected healing and chosen destruction. I always ended with, "I shall never stop praying for you."

At seven o'clock one morning I received an emergency call from my son: "Mom, I am dead serious. This is no lie, Mom. Our apartment is filled with demons. Thousands of them. You gotta come pray over this place."

I didn't try to figure it out. I simply said we were on our way. From past experience I knew I could not count on our pastor, so I called two close friends to go to the apartment with David and me. We wondered whether we would find a drug party and police cars, but the parking lot was devoid of both cars and people.

Lisa sat on the concrete stairs in front of their unit, barefoot and shaking. Scott, barefoot and wild-eyed, came down the stairs toward us. "Mom, we have demons. The apartment is full of them. We've been battling them for hours. I could hardly break away to come out here."

David told the kids to get into the car, not even going back for their shoes. Scott's eyes held the terrified appearance of one who had seen something he should not. Once home we learned what had gone on. There had been a party that lasted for days. After their friends left, weird things happened.

"Something ripped wide open," Scott said. "Demons came. We saw them. We felt them."

"They were everywhere!" Lisa interjected. "We tried grabbing the ones that flew and tossing them out, but they kept coming back. They blocked the front door. We couldn't get out!"

I exchanged incredulous glances with David. They had to have been hallucinating. Yet people are not known to have the very same hallucinations. Lisa, distressed and crying, explained, "We were celebrating Scott's twenty-first birthday Saturday night. Someone brought crystal meth. Then we got into heavy conversation about God and Satan and good and evil and how it's probably best to be good. Sunday morning our friends left, but Scott and I continued talking."

"We talked all day," Lisa continued. "Sunday night I caught shadows in my peripheral vision. Scott saw them too. Then there was no way we could ignore what was happening."

According to Lisa, "things" were in their apartment. Some clear like jellyfish, some flying, some crawling or floating. Some paper thin, some smokylike.

"You were hallucinating," David said.

"No! The air was so thick with them we could not see across the room," Lisa said. "And they made swishy or gurgling sounds. We tried to grab them, to get them out of there. Scott became exhausted and laid down. His eyes were a bright cyan blue, and his pupils were purple. Then Scott got very serious and he said, 'Lisa, you have to do it. You have to ask Jesus Christ into your heart. Right now!'

"After he said it four times, I did. Scott picked up his Bible and began reading out loud. This time when we grabbed at them we said, 'In the name of Jesus get out of here!' And they did. And our fear left us, because God was right there, helping us. But when we touched them, our hands tingled."

Finally Scott spoke up. "And one of them said, *in my own voice,* 'I know you.' And it went on all night, and some ran toward us, and some away, and they had evil, comical grins and as soon as the sun came up, I called you. And I looked out the window and saw a group of men in the parking lot. Maybe they were angels. They were praying."

We had to go back to the apartment, but who else would believe this bizarre tale and go with us to pray? Then I recalled a small, downtown church I had visited years before. Pastor Mark was a godly man, but I had changed churches while looking for one with a larger youth ministry. I opened the phone book to the pastor's name and called.

"You don't know me, but I—we—need help. My son's into drugs. They need help. They saw demons. I don't know what to do…"

Pastor Mark said he could meet us at Scott's apartment at eleven o'clock. As we waited, we discussed what had happened. I said God had placed an invisible barrier between the physical and the spiritual realm that wasn't to be crossed. David agreed. "That's why we feel creepy when we talk about 'ghosts' or the supernatural," he said. "It's like a protection for us to keep us away."

It appeared as though God had lifted the curtain between the two realms to give the kids a good look at forbidden territory. In the Old Testament book of Isaiah, God told the Israelites that because they trusted in their many sorceries, potent spells, and magic spells, disaster would come upon them, and they would not be able to conjure it away. Catastrophe they could not foresee would suddenly come upon them (Isa. 47:9–11). Scott had thought his magic spells would give him power. Yet when disaster came, he was unable to "conjure it away."

Once at the apartment Pastor Mark and his associate pastor went in with us. The atmosphere was dark and oppressive. Paper bats hung from the ceiling. Sweet smells of incense hung over a statue of Buddha. Lisa showed me a brown mark in the shape of a pentagram on the kitchen counter. "We didn't make this," she said. It just appeared. And we've scrubbed it with cleanser and bleach, but it won't come off."

The pastor read scriptures and prayed. He told us that God was sovereign over all things concerning demons. He read from 2 Thessalonians 3:3, "The Lord is faithful, and he will strengthen and protect you from the evil one."

He said Christians have divine power to demolish strongholds, and that we who are in Christ have immunity against the wiles of the devil. Scott and Lisa's lifestyles told him they did not have a personal relationship with Jesus Christ, but maybe God had allowed this experience so they would turn away from evil and receive Jesus.

Lisa dwelled intently upon every word, but Scott took issue with this. "I've done that," he protested. "I already became a Christian a long time ago."

"Then you need to ask God's forgiveness."

"I've done that!" Scott interrupted. "Why don't you believe me?"

The pastor continued, "You need to ask forgiveness for every way you have disobeyed God. You need to toss out your drugs, your beer, your idols. Are you willing to not live together with Lisa?"

Scott angrily replied, "No way!"

When the pastor prayed for them to have the willingness to renounce secret and shameful ways (2 Cor. 4:2), Lisa prayed along with him, acknowledging her desperate need for Jesus Christ. But Pastor Mark said later that Scott "still had the strongholds of darkness on him."

So while I rejoiced over Lisa, who fully committed her life to Christ, I had grave doubts about Scott. He was visibly against our intervention and had refused to pray. *What more could it possibly take for my son to turn to the Lord?* It would take more.

DELIVERANCE

Weeks later Scott and Lisa had a "hippie-type" outdoor wedding, with hippie-type friends and Lisa walking down a sticks-lined aisle barefoot. As the days went by, she grew in her faith, but Scott continued to balk. Although not as severe, more weird things happened in their apartment. I began to lose hope.

I prayed for my son from Psalm 35: "O Lord, how long will you look on? Rescue his life from the ravages, his precious life, from those lions. O Lord, You have seen this. Do not be far from him, O Lord! Awake and rise to his defense! Do not let the enemy think, 'Aha! Just what we wanted!' Or say, 'We have swallowed him up!' But may we shout for joy and gladness, saying, 'The Lord be exalted.'"

Scott and Lisa had to move in with us for a time. Scott left obscure notes on the kitchen message board, such as COPLANAR, AQUA CUPROSA, DAMASK 14c, and EQUIPOTENTIAL 1865. He went for a walk in the state capitol building and saw images in the walls about fractals.

Scott and Lisa moved back into their apartment, then back in with us. He accused his new bride of being pregnant with the devil's child. I could not readmit him to the hospital because he didn't meet the criteria of being "a threat to himself or others."

Lisa and I prayed together against demonic holds over Scott. Once he became angry and tried to bite her. But on another day he opened the Bible, slammed it shut, and broke into sobs, pleading, "Help me! Help me, Jesus!"

I looked him straight in the eye and asked whether he really wanted help. He said yes. Then I asked whether people could come pray for him. He weakly responded, "Yes."

Pastor Mark had come to our aid at a moment's notice, but this whole thing was so scary that I wanted to find someone who was particularly familiar with deliverance. I got on the phone and began calling churches, but even the ones that said they had deliverance ministries wanted nothing to do with this. Then a friend remembered someone who was familiar with demonic interference. I called "JD," and he offered to come to our house that very night.

JD arrived to find David and me, Lisa, two friends, and my daughter Chris gathered in the living room. Scott wandered in and slumped onto the couch. JD began by saying he didn't like the term demon possession. He said it didn't matter whether it was called possession, obsession, compression, repression, or whatever, the devil can be inside, outside, or in the backseat of a car. His point was that despite Scott's claims to have accepted Christ, some sort of attack was taking place, and it had to be dealt with. After we joined him in prayer, JD read Ephesians 6:10–12:

> Be strong in the Lord and in his mighty power. Put on the full armor of God so that you can take your stand against the devil's schemes. For our struggle is not against flesh and blood, but against the rulers, against the authorities, against the powers of this dark world and against the spiritual forces of evil in the heavenly realms.

After an hour of JD talking and praying with my son, Scott became increasingly agitated, intermittently rocking and rubbing his arms. When he finally spoke, it was accusingly and in a voice not his own. When JD told him he needed to renounce his use of marijuana, Scott shouted back, "Do *you* take aspirin?" When JD told him to renounce sexual sin, Scott yelled "Do *you* sleep with your wife?"

JD simply became more authoritative. Then Scott's agitation turned into stark fear. "Are you going to hit me? Kill me?" he asked. He looked at me with terror-stricken eyes, pleading for me to do something. But I closed my eyes against his begging ones and silently prayed, "God, help us."

Scott got up and ducked around the corner so he could grab the phone and call 911. *Someone* had to come to his aid! His sister followed and gently led him back to the living room. Now came loud voices and cries. We prayed aloud, quoting scriptures and praising God for conquering death, hell, and the grave on the cross and having all power. Then Scott abruptly left the room and returned with his Bible. Previously incoherent, he now began speaking clearly and carefully but with a British accent. As Scott read from Revelation, David said, "That's not Scott."

JD demanded that the demon leave. There were more angry cries from Scott. Lisa held his hand. My friend knelt next to him repeating, "Jesus is Lord." The rest of us prayed aloud and sang. Scott paced the room, then lay on the floor in a fetal position, then returned to the couch. JD demanded that Scott be left alone "in the name of Jesus Christ."

At that, Scott tossed his head back and yelled, "Jesus Christ is Lord!" His mouth wide open, Scott let out a terrible roar, and we knew that something had left. It was 11:30 p.m. when we finished our time together by holding hands and singing, "He who began a good work in you will be faithful to complete it in you."

The next morning I found Scott sitting quietly alone in the family room. He looked troubled, saying he'd had a terrible nightmare that someone had tried to kill him. "Scott," I carefully chose my words. "You know that demons have had a heyday with you. It was they who felt threatened. We were there to love you and to help you."

I asked if I could read scriptures to him, and he said yes. A little later he joined us in a big breakfast of waffles and bacon. I encouraged him to do nothing at this time but rest. On our kitchen marker board I wrote, "Today's Rx: God's Word. Prayer. Love. Rest." And that's exactly what he and Lisa did.

"You are fortunate," JD told me over the phone.

"Why on earth?" I asked.

"Because Scott did not have a spirit of murder or suicide or any kind of violence. Only one of insanity." He continued, "Your son is not crazy. He had demonic spirits."

Were there different kinds of evil spirits? I got out my Bible and looked up "spirits" in my concordance. First Samuel 16:14 told of an evil spirit that "tormented" King Saul. First Kings 22:22 told of a "lying spirit." Mark 9:25–29 told of the Lord rebuking a "deaf and mute spirit." But Matthew 8:28 told about "demon possessed men...so violent" that no one could pass by them. Scott did not have that kind of spirit.

With disappointing memories of Pastor Jim and appreciation for Pastor Mark's help, we began attending his church. The assistant pastor who had been with us that day met with Scott every week to help him learn more about the Lord and become grounded in the Scriptures. Good things started happening. David and I came home from dinner out one night to find Scott and Lisa laughing themselves silly over an old *Dennis the Menace* movie. Lisa said that before the movie Scott had read out of the Book of Hebrews, and it helped him. We all sat down to coffee and cheesecake.

It was time for the newlyweds to clean up their old apartment and move back in. Scott could not bring himself to go near it but asked Lisa to haul all the drug paraphernalia to our place. As soon as she returned, he dragged the heavy boxes into our driveway and spilled the contents. There was an amazing collection of bongs, pipes, blackened spoons, CO_2 cartridges from sniffing nitrous oxide, books on quantum physics, drug-related magazines, and music tapes by bands such as The Thrill Kill Kult. He attacked the items with a vengeance, stomping and smashing until they lay in an ungodly mess on the concrete. The destruction was punctuated by Scott's yelling and sobbing. Then he went inside and collapsed on the couch.

The next day dawned sunny and warm. I awoke to hear Scott and Lisa laughing in their room. After reading the Bible together, they walked a mile to a state park where they collected heart-shaped stones from the beach. In my diary I wrote, "Lord, let the healing continue."

The following day Scott said he had been reading a little book given him by a friend called *Now That I Believe*. We discussed the part in 2 Chronicles that says God will fight our battles for us. It wasn't long until Scott became the first one ready for church. He listened carefully to the sermon and sang, "Lord I lift my hands to You. I'm so glad You're in my life. I'm so glad You came to save me."

On Sunday evenings he and Lisa attended a young couples Bible study held in a private home. Members from our new church reached out to them in many ways. Anonymous cards with twenty-dollar bills appeared in their mailbox. Sacks of groceries were left. One time a package left on their doorstep contained a new set of flannel sheets, accompanied by a check for two hundred dollars.

For the rest of the summer we asked only that the two continue to rest and heal. They planted an herb garden and set up tubs for tie-dying T-shirts. Lisa showed me how to make bead necklaces. When friends invited us water-skiing, Scott proved his former agility by staying on one ski all over the lake.

One day after listening to a call-in program on Christian radio, he called and told them that God is the only One who can get a person free from drugs. Both of the kids knew they had to cut off contact with old friends. This proved to be easier than they thought. In Lisa's words, "I told everyone that Scott was afflicted by demons and Jesus set him free. After that they wanted nothing more to do with us."

However, when an acquaintance of theirs was admitted to the psychiatric ward, Scott was quick to go visit. Unruffled by his friend's talk of how he could make the lights flicker by blinking his eyes, Scott told him that he himself was once in the room across the hall. "I heard those voices too. Would you like me to pray with you?"

"Mom, I just praised God," Scott told me later, "because I was back there in the psych ward, but this time I was on the other side."

I thought my joy couldn't be any greater until the day Lisa walked into the room smiling, saying she and Scott had an important place to go and asked if they could they use my car. "Hmm," I murmured, "I guess so. Where are you going?"

Lisa laughed. "Are you ready for this? We're going to a place that offers free pregnancy tests."

The test was positive. I cherish the photo I have of their infant son Noah watching his mommy and daddy being baptized in the river. Scott found a full-time job working the swing shift, and he attended community college during the day, where he earned his associate's degree. In time Scott and Lisa would become the parents of not one but five children.

It had been a long haul. Why so long? Because once Scott began heavy drug use, it led him right into practicing the occult. The occult opened the door to demons. The demonic influence led him straight into insanity.

All believers contend with invisible forces on a spiritual battle-field. In fact, in Ephesians 6:12 the apostle Paul warns, "We wrestle not against flesh and blood, but against principalities, against powers, against the rulers of the darkness of this world, against spiritual wickedness in high places" (KJV). Paul also assures us that we can overcome them by putting on (the spiritual) armor of God (Eph. 6:13).

Due to his own foolishness, Scott allowed his mind and spirit to become badly damaged, rendering him unable to respond to God's help. As a mom, I praise God that He gave me the privilege of inter-vening on my son's behalf and engaging in warfare *for* him through prayer, believing the Scriptures, patient perseverance, and trusting the power of our almighty God.

There is no darkness too thick for the light to penetrate.

RECOMMENDED RESOURCES

- *Escape From the Fowler's Snare* by Karen Strand (Wine Press Publishing, 2000)

- *Occult Bondage and Deliverance* by Kurt Koch (Kregel, 1970)

- *Occult Practices and Beliefs* by Kurt Koch (Kregel, 1971)

- *Evil and Human Suffering* by Walter Martin, CD/ audiotape (Walter Martin Ministries, www .waltermartin.com)

- *Growing in the Spirit* by Walter Martin, CD/ audiotape (Walter Martin Ministries, www .waltermartin.com)

- *The Kingdom of the Occult* by Walter Martin, Jill Martin Rische, and Kurt Van Gorden (Thomas Nelson, 2008)

Carol Carlson is a freelance writer whose articles and poems have appeared in a wide range of publications. She and her husband live in the Pacific Northwest, where they enjoy their six grown children and more than a dozen grandchildren.

CONCLUSION

WHEN I STARTED this book, I wanted to give the reader an understanding of who occultists are, what they practice, how to effectively reach them, and how some have found freedom in Christ. Once the writing process began and I started to read through my testimony and the stories of the contributing authors, I was overcome by the reality of God's involvement in people's lives even when they were rebelling against Him. In writing this, I can see that God actively pursues individuals in His love for them.

Occultists have contacted me and shared how God intervened in their lives while they were performing a ritual to another god. Truly "God so loved the world that he gave his one and only Son, that whoever believes in him shall not perish but have eternal life. For God did not send his Son into the world to condemn the world, but to save the world through him" (John 3:16–17). Satan may be prowling like a lion seeking whom he may devour (1 Pet. 5:8), but God is pouring out His kindness, which leads us to repentance (Rom. 2:4).

I hope that as you read these chapters, you came to understand that many occultists are simply seeking the truth. It is God's heart to reach them. He might even want to use you.

WHO THE OCCULTIST IS

Remember, the occultist is simply a human being whom God has created. And God loves each one of them. Every human being created by God has a hole in his heart that only God can fill. That need for a relationship with God is what drives the occultist; it is what he is looking for in his practice of hidden knowledge.

As Christians who know the love of God, we need to help the occultist find what he truly seeks. Before I was born again, I encountered Christians who knew I was practicing Satanism yet never told me I was going to hell, condemned me, or came across with an attitude that said, "I'm right; you're wrong." They simply told me that Jesus loved me, and it was exactly that kindness from God that led me to repentance.

It's not easy to befriend people headed toward hell and not take them by the shoulders and shake them until they see the truth. But open confrontation seldom works. We need to help them see who God is through our actions. Nothing will express who God is more than love. Remember, God *is* love. Indeed this love embraces both God's judgment and His righteousness. Yet when it comes to the way we connect with people, it must be through the fruit of the Holy Spirit: "love, joy, peace, patience, kindness, goodness, faithfulness, gentleness and self-control" (Gal. 5:22–23). Showing the love and character of God will make the strongest impact on the occultist, not our words of condemnation.

Amber Rane explained very clearly in chapter 2 the inner world of an occultist: how they see things, how they think, and what they feel. When you connect with someone who is in the occult, remember that you are dealing with someone who is overcome with darkness. Be the light that will bring them life.

What Occultists Practice

If you are going to minister to people in the occult, it is imperative that you have at least a general understanding of where they've been. Never assume that you know what they practice or impose your beliefs on them. For example, if you come across someone who practices Wicca, which is a very popular form of paganism today, and tell the person he worships the devil, that individual likely will think you don't know what you're talking about. Of course, from your perspective his *is* worshipping the devil, but you must meet the person where his is.

Many occultists have stopped dialoguing with well-meaning Christians because those believers said too much too soon. I encourage you to just listen. Consider what that person sees and share the truth with him in love, slowly and gently.

Laura Maxwell did a tremendous job explaining what spiritualists believe and practice and how the occultist can easily move from one practice to another. In the world of the occult, truth is relative. As long as a belief or practice works, the occultist will take it and run with it and still call himself Wiccan, pagan, Druid, or whatever he wants.

The occultist is on a spiritual journey, just as we are, and he will try to find truth anywhere he can. The good news is that as Christians, we know the truth that will set the occultist free (John 8:31–32). (If you want to learn more about the various occult practices, no one explains this topic better than Walter Martin, his daughter Jill Martin Rische, and Kurt Van Gorden in their book, *The Kingdom of the Occult.* I highly recommend this resource.)

HOW TO REACH THE OCCULTIST

Let's say you know someone at work who is a practicing witch. What's the very first thing you would do to reach out to him? Invite him to church or Bible study? Confront him about the pentagram around his neck? I would recommend that you pray for that person and that you submit yourself to God and to be used to reflect His character. That way, the witch in your office might see the truth that will set him free.

Of course, it's natural to want to run up and tell an occultist that he's in darkness and you know the way out. But rather than frightening or offending the person with our enthusiasm, we need to simply model Christ to him every day. Remember, God is the one pursuing the occultist, not you. You are simply a vessel He will use to reflect His love and goodness.

Meet people where they are. Enter into their world. You would be surprised how many people need someone to listen to them and care about them. The best way I have found to enter into someone else's world is to show him I can be trusted. I don't come in talking first, telling him what he's doing wrong and how he needs to get right with God. I come in with my ears and my heart open. This gives the person a chance to see me as a loving, caring human being. If people feel they can trust you, they will eventually disclose their need. Then they can be introduced to the One who can satisfy their longings.

Ministering to the Occultist

When a person renounces the occult, what happens next? As I said before, the phrase "to minister" means to provide for the needs of another. So what does this new believer need?

That will depend upon the individual. As a Christian who has entered into their world, you, first and foremost, need to be there for them. You will need to be faithful to support them through whatever they are facing while, again, reflecting Christ's character. Sometimes in addition to their spiritual needs, people will have practical needs. Feed them dinner, pick them up for church, listen to them, pray for them, and direct them back to God when they think their world is falling apart.

Please understand, they have just left everything they have known, everything that made them feel significant. They have humbled themselves like a child (Matt. 18:4) and been born again (John 3:3), and now all things have become new (2 Cor. 5:17). But this new path is unfamiliar, and they will need both guidance and friendship.

Find a Bible for them that they can understand and allow them to ask you questions. But be careful not to overwhelm them with too many Christian resources. You may be tempted to shower the new believer with Christian "stuff," but it is important that you don't replace occult paraphernalia with Christian paraphernalia. Allow the person to learn how to commune peacefully with God. Recommend, however, that he clear his house of everything related to the occult. It will be time for a fresh start.

Now let's address the fact that these former occultists have been interacting with the demonic realm. You may find that in leading someone to Christ, he or she is demonized. When I went to dinner at Harry and Jo's house, they had no idea they would need to cast anything out of me. So be prepared. A former occultist may need deliverance.

This is nothing to fear. I have met many Christians who will not take the necessary steps to help someone who has been involved in the occult because they fear the power of the demonic. We are instructed in Scripture to only fear God. "The fear of the Lord is the beginning of wisdom, and knowledge of the Holy One is understanding" (Prov. 9:10).

We need to realize that the God we serve is *the Almighty*. He said in His Word, "I will be a Father to you, and you will be my sons and daughters, says the Lord Almighty" (2 Cor. 6:18). *Almighty* comes from the Greek word *pantokrator*, which means "He rules over all." If you are a son or daughter of God, you too rule over the demonic power of the occult. This is simply a result of your position in Christ.

Ephesians 2:6 says, "God raised us up with Christ and seated us with him in the heavenly realms in Christ Jesus." We have this authority because of what Christ did on the cross, not because of anything we have done. We can have confidence that He who is in us is greater than he who is in the world (1 John 4:4). We have no reason to be afraid.

You may also find that the person you are helping is in need of healing—healing of the mind, healing of emotions, healing of memories, healing of many kinds. The individual may find himself crying without knowing why. This isn't necessarily a bad thing. Crying may be evidence of a heart that is being softened and feeling something for the first time in a long time. Yet the person could be dealing with any number of issues. This is why it is important that we don't get caught up in following a particular discipleship method but rather that we look to Jesus for wisdom, because He can heal every condition:

> You know what has happened through Judea, beginning in Galilee after the baptism that John preached—how God anointed Jesus of Nazareth with the Holy Spirit and power, and how he went around doing good and healing all who were under the power of the devil, because God was with him.
>
> —ACTS 10:37–38

A FINAL WORD

Through this book I have tried to give you understanding and equip you for action. My friends and I wrote this resource so you could know the specific needs of someone who is in or coming out of the occult and be able to offer him spiritual and practical help. But by no means is this volume exhaustive.

I thank God for those in the body of Christ who already are helping people leave the occult, but God is calling many more. Maybe you're one of them. We certainly hope so. Remember, you are not alone. My friends and I are here to help you. If you are ministering to someone who has come out of the occult, or if you have been involved in the occult yourself and are looking for someone to talk with who understands and cares, we welcome your questions. You can contact us at info@refugeministries.cc.

Be blessed.

NOTES

CHAPTER 1
FROM DEMON HABITATION TO TEMPLE OF THE HOLY SPIRIT

1. Walter Martin, Jill Martin Rische, and Kurt Van Gorden, *The Kingdom of the Occult* (Nashville, TN: Thomas Nelson, 2008).

CHAPTER 2
A SATANIST WHO GREW UP IN CHURCH

1. Adolf Hitler Quotes, ThinkExist.com, http://thinkexist.com/quotation/make_the_lie_big-make_it_simple-keep_saying_it/175795.html (accessed March 8, 2012).

CHAPTER 5
THE REALITY OF CHRISTIAN WITCHCRAFT

1. "I believe he [Jesus] was a Witch. He worked miracles or what we would call magic, cured people and did most things expected from a Witch. He had his coven of thirteen." Quoted from Arnold Crowther and Patricia Crowther, *The Secrets of Ancient Witchcraft With the Witches Tarot* (Secaucus, NJ: University Books, 1974), 164.

2. Martin, Rische, and Van Gorden, *The Kingdom of the Occult*.

3. I recommend the following article, which discusses the need for Christians to evangelize Wiccans. Josh Kimball, "Wicca Experts Encourage Christians to Engage America's 'Fastest-Growing' Religion," *The Christian Post*, September 21, 2008, http://www.christianpost.com/news/wicca-experts-encourage-christians-to-engage-america-s-fastest-growing-religion-34408/ (accessed March 21, 2012).

CHAPTER 6
FROM SPIRITUALISM TO CHRIST

1. B. F. Austin, *The A.B.C. of Spiritualism* (Milwaukee, WI: National Spiritualist Association of Churches, n.d.), 23.

2. Josh McDowell and Don Stewart, *Handbook of Today's Religions* (San Bernardino, CA: Here's Life Publishers, Inc., 1983).

3. David Spangler, *Reflections on the Christ*, revised edition (Everett, WA: Lorian Press, 1978).

4. David Spangler, *Reflections on the Christ* (Forres, Scotland: Findhorn Publications, 1981), 43, 45; Benjamin Creme, *The Ageless Wisdom Teaching* (London: Share International Foundation, 1996, 2006), 42.

5. Kevin Logan, *Paganism and the Occult*, (n.p.: Kingsway Publications, 1994), 126

6. Ben Alexander, *Out From Darkness* (Elmsford, NY: Miranda Press, 2005), 84.

CHAPTER 8
FREED FROM SATAN'S GRASP

1. Martin, Rische, and Van Gorden, *The Kingdom of the Occult.*

2. Vivianne Crowley writes in her book *Wicca*: "All the religious and magical practices on which the Catholic Church did not bestow its blessings—other Christian sects, Paganism, and magic—were now lumped together. Whatever their aims and virtues, they were declared to be Devil worship.... Despite fierce attempts to persecute those Christians whose views did not accord with Catholicism, the heretical sects which later transmuted into the Protestant movement flourished and grew strong." (Vivianne Crowley, *Wicca*, revised and updated ed. [Salisbury, England: Element Books, 2003], 19-20).

3. The title of Norman L. Geisler and William E. Nix's *A General Introduction to the Bible* (Chicago: Moody Publishers, 1986) is somewhat misleading, as it is actually quite a comprehensive study but excellent for those wanting to study in depth. For those wanting a more brief overview, I recommend the booklet *Knowing the Truth About the Reliability of the Bible* by John Ankerberg and John Weldon (Harvest House Publishers, 1998).

CHAPTER 10
DEMON POSSESSION—A MOTHER'S STORY

1. Martin, Rische, and Van Gorden, *The Kingdom of the Occult.*

ABOUT REFUGE MINISTRIES

REFUGE MINISTRIES WAS born out of need. There are count-less people who have loved ones involved in the occult and countless others who have been involved themselves. Many are looking for a ministry that will gently reach out to them and take their need seriously without making them feel like outcasts.

When I was a struggling Satanist, the Lord sent certain people into my life to minister to me. Through their involvement in my life, I was given the help I needed to be set free from Satanism. The Bible tells us, "Freely you have received, freely give" (Matt. 10:8). Now it is our heart's desire to help you in any way that we can. That is why Refuge Ministries was created.

If you have been involved in Satanism, the occult, Wicca, witch-craft, New Age practices, or false teachings in the Christian church, we are here to help you. We offer biblical counsel, prayer, encour-agement, and resources. You are welcome to contact us for any reason at www.refugeministries.cc or info@refugeministries.cc.